# SONG OF THE BARREN
## MISCARRIAGES TO MIRACLES

Michelle Renée Chudy

KINGDOM KINETIC
— *Publishing* —

*Song of the Barren*
Copyright © 2018 by Michelle Renée Chudy. All rights reserved.
This title is also available as an ebook.

No part of this publication may be reproduced, stored in a retrieval system or transmitted in any way by any means, electronic, mechanical, photocopy, recording or otherwise without the prior permission of the author except as provided by USA copyright law.
Scripture quotations taken from the Amplified® Bible (AMP),
Copyright © 2015 by The Lockman Foundation
Used by permission. www.Lockman.org
Scripture quotations marked (CSB) are taken from *The Christian Standard Bible.* The Christian Standard Bible. Copyright © 2017 by Holman Bible Publishers. Used by permission. Christian Standard Bible®, and CSB® are federally registered trademarks of Holman Bible Publishers, all rights reserved.
Scripture quotations marked (NKJV) are taken from the *New King James Version®*.
Scripture taken from the New King James Version®. Copyright © 1982 by Thomas Nelson. Used by permission. All rights reserved.
Scripture quotations marked (NIV) are taken from the *Holy Bible, New International Version®*. THE HOLY BIBLE, NEW INTERNATIONAL VERSION®, NIV® Copyright © 1973, 1978, 1984, 2011 by Biblica, Inc.® Used by permission. All rights reserved worldwide.
Scripture quotations marked (NLT) are taken from the Holy Bible, New Living Translation, copyright © 1996, 2004, 2007, 2013, 2015 by Tyndale House Foundation. Used by permission of Tyndale House Publishers, Inc., Carol Stream, Illinois 60188. All rights reserved.

Published by Kingdom Kinetic Publishing
2913 Gateway Park Lane, Lexington, KY 40511 USA
1.859.429.1727| www.michellechudy.com
Kingdom Kinetic Publishing is committed to excellence in the publishing industry. The company promotes from the heart good matter from the pens of His ready writers who have the call to arise and shine for His glory is upon them.
"*My heart is indicting a good matter: I speak of the things which I have made touching the king: my tongue is the pen of a ready writer*" (Psalm 45:1 KJB).
"*Arise, shine; For your light has come! And the glory of the Lord is risen upon you. For behold, the darkness shall cover the earth, and deep darkness the people; But the Lord will arise over you, and His glory will be seen upon you. The Gentiles shall come to your light, and kings to the brightness of your rising.* (Isaiah 60:1-3 NKJV).
Book design copyright © 2018 by Michelle Chudy Enterprises, LLC. All rights reserved.
*Cover & Interior Design: Michelle Chudy*
*Front Cover Photography: Charley's Angels Premier Newborn Hospital Photography*
*Back Cover Photography: Jennifer Palumbo*
*Interior Photography: Michelle Chudy, Jennifer Palumbo*

Published in the United States of America
ISBN-13: 978-0-9976989-3-0 (Print)
ISBN-13: 978-0-9976989-5-4 (eBook)

18.03.05

# Dedication

This book is dedicated with an everlasting love, from all my being, to each of my children both earth and heaven born...Haidyn Elise, John Mark, Abigail Annalise, Caris Sophia, and the babe yet to come. You have taught me the beauty of life and how to live full-hearted as a mother. Most importantly, you showed me the love of the heavenly Father, and my Lord and Savior Jesus Christ.

Not only are you my legacy, but my gifts to the future. You are earthly tabernacles of the Living God. It's an honor to be called your momma. You are cherished. Live and love well my blessings! Know who you are in Christ, walk in your authentic identity, live your purpose, and rock this world for Jesus. Arise, and shine!

Love,

Momma/MomMom

# Acknowledgements

**Abba**, thank You for remembering me and the cries of my heart. Thank You for not listening to my prayers which were lifted in fear asking not to be pregnant again. Thank You, **Jesus**, for my beautiful, baby girl Caris Sophia and a healed heart! Thank You, **Holy Spirit**, for Your comfort, strength and dunamis power that brings even a dead womb back to life. Who am I LORD, that You would remember me? I am truly grateful.

Many thanks to each contributor whom so graciously shared their story to amplify my Song and God's healing through testimony. **Pastor Mark** and **Katie Keene**, **Rebecca Blackburn**, **Jennifer Plummer**, **Krystal Strasser**, **Jordan Sanders**, **Kevin Sheehan** and **Hope Beryl-Green**, it's with a humble heart and deep gratitude that I thank each of you for the honor and privilege of sharing your story. Thank you for entrusting me with the precious memory and treasure of your heaven born babes.

**Mark Chudy**, my husband of twenty-five years, father of my children, and life partner for better or worse. This chapter of our story brought much sorrow and joy. Somethings we do well, others not so much. But no one can argue that we make beautiful children together, inside and out. Here's to you, to infinity and beyond, where John Mark and Abigail await our family reunion beyond heaven's gates. You are a blessed man indeed.

**Haidyn Elise** – My True Love Girl – I love you more than you can ever know. I stand in awe of the woman of God you are becoming. You are the best Sissy and the sweetest example of Jesus in this world. Thank you for letting the world see into your big, beautiful heart of sister love, so those who need it can learn and heal from your grief. Haidyn, your stunning exterior pales in comparison to the loveliness that dwells within. You make me so proud to be your momma.

**Mr. and Mrs. Jim Mitchell** – I thank Jesus for the sweet relationship and friendship that filled a void in all our lives. Jim, you are deeply missed and thought of often! Each memory brings a smile. You were the recipient of Caris' first word, "hi". I contribute her social-butterfly ways to you, as well as her fascination with sports. Lillian a.k.a. "Grammie" thank you for blessing us in so many ways…too many to count. I love you for every doting moment poured out on our kids. For every Oreo, Teddy Graham teachable moment, ice cream and cheese nights, family dinners, and most of all for being you!

**Audrey Anderson** and **Sonia Rios**, all these years later, your kindness and tenderness expressed during our loss still makes my heart warm. When others didn't understand, your love pushed passed my walls and ministered to my soul. Thank you for acknowledging my grief and providing comfort with meals for my family. Love you both to heaven and back!

**Dr. Elizabeth Elkinson**, you are the best of the best and the perfect one to assist in bringing our miracle into the world. Not only do I appreciate your exceptional medical knowledge and skills, but more importantly your heart and compassion. Thank you for being human. Thank you for listening, accommodating my needs, honoring my wishes and being considerate of my fears. There is no doubt you were God-appointed and a blessing.

**Prophet Ed Traut**, a true prophet edifies the body of Christ with their prophetic word. And that is exactly what you did, and consistently do, for our family. Thank you for your faithfulness and obedience in delivering His proclamation of our miracle. You equipped me to not only warfare but live in peace and rejoice instead of fear. May the blessing you bestowed on me come back to you in double portion.

Prophetic Life Ministries, San Antonio, Texas. www.propheticlife.com

**Jennifer Palumbo a.k.a. the Baby Whisperer**, our wildly talented photographer. I'm so grateful that the blessing of Caris opened the door to meet you. You have beautifully captured the moments, milestones, sass and humor of this now pint-sized dynamo. Love your work girl!

Baby Boo Photography & Studio B2, Nicholasville, Kentucky. www.babyboophotography.com

# Table of Contents

Dedication ..................................................................... i

Acknowledgements ...................................................... ii

Table of Contents ......................................................... v

Foreword ................................................................... viii

*My Story* ..................................................................... 1

Prologue ...................................................................... 2

   Though He Loves Me ............................................... 12

   A Time to Mourn ..................................................... 14

      Chapter 1 - A Shattered Heart ............................ 15

   Too Tired to Breathe ............................................... 42

      Chapter 2 - Fool Me Twice .................................. 44

      Chapter 3 - Love Has a Name .............................. 49

      Chapter 4 - Sissy Love…Haidyn's Letter .............. 52

   Well of Barrenness .................................................. 54

      Chapter 5 - The Place Between ........................... 55

   A Time to Believe .................................................... 58

      Chapter 6 - Cramps and Cravings ........................ 59

      Chapter 7 - Blessed Assurance ............................ 64

      Chapter 8 - A Well-Timed Word .......................... 68

      Chapter 9 - The Big Reveal .................................. 71

      Chapter 10 - Look Momma! ................................ 73

Chapter 11 - It's a Girl! ............................................. 78

Chapter 12 - Whispers from Heaven ................... 81

Chapter 13 - Coaxed by Love ................................ 85

Chapter 14 - No Shopping Shame! ...................... 90

Chapter 15 - Showered with Sissy Love .............. 93

Chapter 16 - A Time to Wait ................................. 96

Chapter 17 – Caris Eve... The Last Night of Chudy-Three .......................................................... 98

*A Time to Sing* ............................................................... 104

Chapter 18 - Labor of Love ................................. 105

Chapter 19 - The Father's Hand ........................ 109

Chapter 20 – Introducing... Caris Sophia Chudy ................................................................... 111

Chapter 21 - The Stocking ................................. 112

Chapter 22 - Holy Visitations ............................. 114

Chapter 23 - Great Expectations ....................... 118

A Gift ....................................................................... 122

*His Heart* ...................................................................... 123

*Their Story* .................................................................... 133

A Time to Be Comforted ..................................... 134

*Your Story* .................................................................... 162

Time to Heal ......................................................... 163

Grief Healing Exercises ....................................... 166

The Healing Journey ........................................... 168

| | |
|---|---|
| You're Invited | 173 |
| Your Notes | 175 |
| Resources | 176 |
| Afterword | 178 |
| Author's Note | 182 |
| Notes to Text | 186 |

# Foreword

*"Rejoice, barren one, who did not give birth; burst into song and shout, you who have not been in labor! For the children of the forsaken one will be more than the children of the married woman," says the Lord. Isaiah 54:1 (CSB)*

I have seen the word of God fulfilled! My twelve years of barrenness were a blessing and not a curse. I was chosen to see the supernatural and the glory of God, and to be the carrier of a miracle. Because of stored prayers kept in the heart of my Father, I received yet another wonder...*His* miracle, and her name is Caris Sophia Chudy.

FIGURE 1: CARIS SOPHIA CHUDY
4 MONTHS YOUNG

## Prologue

So...imagine my surprise when I finally go to the dr, convinced that I'm starting menopause, and discover that I'm 10 WEEKS PREGNANT!! That was almost four weeks ago!

Mark, Haidyn and I are blessed to announce the projected arrival of a little Chudy on or around August 20, 2013! SURPRISE!!!

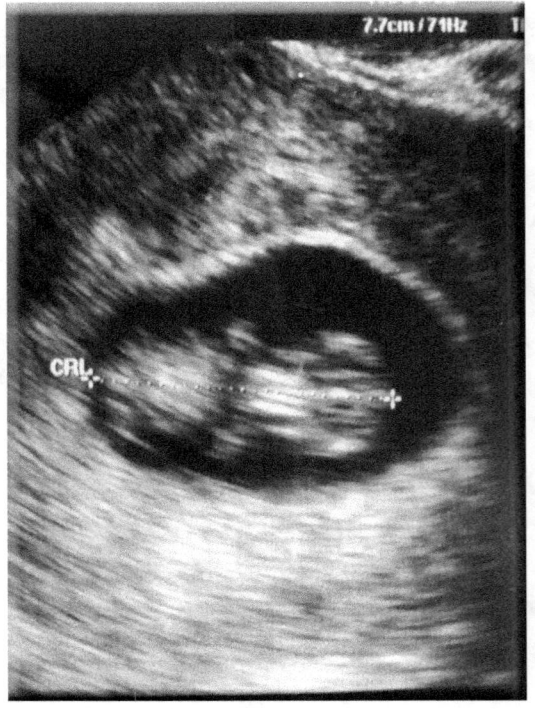

FIGURE 2: CARIS SOPHIA'S 1ST ULTRASOUND

Posted on February 14th - Valentine's Day - this was my most-liked Facebook post of the year. The day of announcement was strategically chosen. I wanted it to be a special surprise for my daughter Haidyn while announcing the big reveal.

Haidyn wanted to be a big sister so badly. She was almost twelve and had prayed for years for a little sister or brother. Hidden under all the other Valentine's presents was the *I'm Going to be a Big Sister* t-shirt. It was the last gift in her bag.

If I am to be completely transparent, fear helped me pick the date. It eased us two weeks past the first trimester and into a sigh of relief. Mark and I would be forty-five when the baby was due. This pregnancy was high risk, and age was just one of the factors.

Truth be told, this wasn't the first big-sister shirt for Haidyn. There is one a few sizes smaller, which she has never seen, tucked away in my blanket chest. It is hidden away with the only ultrasound picture and a positive pregnancy test that serve as proof of the baby's life...Haidyn's first sibling. These are the tangibles that tether my soul to a child that I've never met. They connect me to a pain so primal it stripped my heart bare.

And then one year later, almost to the day, I was reintroduced to that pain again after a brief lapse of hope. As quickly as I realized I was pregnant again, those few days of timid joy were soon drenched with another storm of miscarriage tears. I lost another baby.

There was no ultrasound picture this time, or heartbreaking D&C like the last. I only had the positive pregnancy test and six weeks of symptoms to verify the baby's life. The previously scheduled doctor's appointment to determine a due date confirmed death and not life.

The pain was different the second time. The tears flowed, but they didn't resemble the tempest fueled by loss, like with the first baby. My heart seemed to shrink after the second loss. I think hope left that day or maybe it leaked out over the following years of barrenness.

When I lost the first baby, I tried to console the grief and anger with reason. Guarding my heart was critical, if I was to survive without the poison of bitterness in my soul. Since I served as a life coach in a ministry at my church, I thought maybe God let me walk the path of miscarriage, so I could understand the pain. If I knew the pain, it would better equip me to help others who also dealt with the same kind of grief. I realized after the first loss, that most people don't know how to help, let alone support someone grieving from miscarriage. Since in most circumstances there is no one to bury, they expect you to get along with life like the death or baby never happened…as if the baby never lived.

And then without an explanation in which to wrap my mind and heart, a year later I was back at the same place of loss, with the same questions, and the same familiar gripping pain. A grief so heavy, it restricts breathing. *How could I explain it? Once was horrible, but twice? How could God let me go through it again?* It was almost like playing the fool because I believed I would never have to feel that way again. I trusted the Lord and assumed my trust would exempt me from the trial, especially a trial that I had just barely survived. The wounds were still fresh. They were tender when pressed. I felt betrayed. Betrayed by a God who promised to never leave nor forsake me. I felt forsaken.

If I had to describe myself based on instinctual behaviors, I'm a survivalist. I normally learn my lessons quickly and avoid the same pain at all cost; especially, the lessons where I'm badly burned. Building emotional walls for protection is my natural response. And since I tend to be an overachiever, mine are more like a fortress. However, I had spent three years prior to the first miscarriage tearing down ungodly strongholds from around my heart. I learned through counseling how damaging it is to live trapped in emotional isolation with a hard heart. The walls not only prevent pain, they also restrict joy and all other healthy emotions.

But with the loss of two babies, my emotions were raw, and trust was exhausted. Hope became a myth. My heart seemed better tended by not being placed out there with expectation for another child. When I hoped for a miracle, I got an emotional beating instead. Miscarriage felt like the punishment for wishing, so I stopped.

I soon found myself praying not to be pregnant. *I wasn't ready yet.* Truthfully, it wasn't the baby I didn't want. It was the possibility of miscarriage. I lacked the faith to get me through the fear. I lacked the energy to hope. I was tormented by the taunting possibility of another death. It was safer not to hope and to quit praying. My hat goes off to those of you who persevered past the pain and kept trying after multiple losses. Two was enough to make me a quitter.

A perpetual analyzer, my thoughts churned as they plagued me. *Maybe I was only supposed to have just one child...maybe I was a bad mom to Haidyn and didn't deserve another baby...maybe this was punishment for me not keeping my promises to God when I was single.* There were so many "maybes" they scratched at the corners of my mind and whispered behind my back, as if I couldn't hear them. And last, but not least was the plaguing, *Did I do something to deserve this?*

Having children was never a sure thing for me. Chances were slim from the beginning. With a suspected history of endometriosis and only one ovary, Mark and I were never sure if I would be able to get pregnant. Surprisingly and with much relief, Haidyn was conceived within six months. This was after nine years of marriage and at the age of thirty-two. My pregnancy with Haidyn was considered high risk due to age, placenta previa and gestational diabetes, but overall it was an easy, text-book pregnancy. The worst part was the heartburn.

Since the conception and pregnancy of Haidyn went so well, I thought we dodged the fertility and miscarriage issues. Eight years later, I was still totally convinced miscarriage wasn't an option since we got pregnant so easily the first time. I believed God wouldn't allow it because He had just worked a miracle for me to get pregnant again. I was shattered when He did. The baby died somewhere around seven weeks.

And then a year later, I was surprised by another positive pregnancy test. My mindset wasn't quite as steadfast as before, but I trusted that I was exempt from another miscarriage. *A loving God wouldn't make me suffer again, right?* Around six weeks the cramping started, and I knew. As much as I tried to stop it with my will to believe and constant prayer, it wasn't enough. The baby was gone.

As the years moved on, the pain eased. I sealed it off in its own little emotional coffin by not thinking about it. The solitary moments of wailing transitioned to occasional sobs; however, it was the mental barricade to the memories that successfully dammed the tears. Only misty eyes would show up, if I started in that direction. Infants were kept at a distance because they evoked yearning for what I lost. Baby showers, baby stores and all baby items were avoided. I wouldn't even let myself look. I could feel the hard, cold wall come down inside of me when I happened to glance their way. They taunted me and made me feel ashamed because I couldn't measure up to their use. Apathy moved in along with numbness of heart. It didn't hurt because I wouldn't let it. I suffocated my heart's cries until it stopped wrestling with longing for something I couldn't have.

This resolve was in place when unknowingly I found myself positioned for a miracle. I had literally moved on to a new job in a different state with a renewed life focus. I was content with my beautiful, one-and-only child. Then seven months after accepting my new position, I started to have flu symptoms when I got back from a business trip.

On the flight there, a lady sitting near me coughed for hours. I just knew one of the germs must have gotten to me.

I recovered after a couple of days at home but continued to have random symptoms. Then abdominal cramping started, and I just felt miserable.

Convinced I was starting menopause, I set an appointment to meet with my new OBGYN to beg for hormones. I took the next appointment available even though it was two weeks away. A coworker jokingly asked if I was pregnant. I didn't think it was funny, let alone plausible. Mark and I had gone without contraceptives for a couple of years to no avail. I just assumed it wasn't going to happen. I was forty-four and past the stage of hoping for a baby. Haidyn was almost twelve. It seemed impossible.

A few days later with my coworker's question tap dancing in my head, I got suspicious when I started to crave orange juice. It was the one thing I craved when pregnant with Haidyn that tipped me over the gestational diabetic edge, early in the first trimester. Not wanting to say anything to Mark, I picked up a pregnancy test after church that Sunday.

When everyone headed off for their Sunday afternoon nap, I snuck off and took the test. *It was positive!* I didn't know what to think, let alone feel. It was like my emotions were coming out from under anesthesia - confused, pained, and firing in all directions. It was hope and dread at the same time. I didn't want anyone to know until the doctor confirmed the test. That mistake was made before by announcing the pregnancy too soon, then having to inform everyone that I miscarried. On top of unimaginable grief, my unwavering faith in God's protection and miscarriage exemption made me feel foolish in the light of reality.

I decided I would at least show Mark the test. He should know first and then I would call the doctor in the morning. So, with test in hand, I showed Mark the results. He was excited and said it was an answer to prayer. Stunned, I had no idea he was still praying for another child. I had stopped praying and believing years ago.

The next day, I made the call to the doctor's office and explained my situation. Without hesitation, they moved up my appointment. Because of my history, the nurse moved quickly to get me in for an ultrasound.

As I laid there on the table in the doctor's office waiting for the equipment to arrive, I tried not to think of the last time I was in this situation... *August 31, 2009. It was the appointment to find out the due date of the first baby. The doctor tried to find a heartbeat but kept searching in silence. There wasn't one...*This time as I waited, I distracted myself from the unwanted memory by conversing with the current nurse and doctor, since it was my first time meeting them.

After what seemed like an eternity, they were finally ready for the ultrasound. Lost in my own side of the conversation, I heard the doctor say, "There is one *very* active baby in there! You're measuring ten weeks pregnant." Her words seem to be delayed in the atmosphere. They took a few seconds to hit my ears and sink in after they were said. *I'm ten weeks pregnant?!* I made it past both time-markers of pregnancy that were insurmountable for my miscarried babies. I don't believe finding out at ten weeks was happenstance.

Cautiously optimistic, Mark and I decided to wait past the first trimester before we told anyone. After looking at the calendar, we chose Valentine's Day as our reveal date. Our little secret was growing while held in confidence between Mark, me and the doctor's office.

The next week, we attended a conference at our church where our secret was almost outed. It never occurred to me to ask the Lord to keep quiet about His miraculous handiwork until we were comfortable to tell.

The church was hosting a prophecy conference. The speaker asked, "How many kids do you have and are you expecting more?" Not wanting to lie, especially in church, I hedged with my answer. Within minutes, the man spoke what we already knew, but hadn't told a soul. He said we would have another baby. The baby was a supernatural intervention of God.

Floored, I just sat there strangely comforted by his words. Those words would bring much peace during times of fear over the next six months. They are part of the reason for writing this book. This book is my thank you and offering to God for His miracle and to give Him glory. I know that I am to comfort others who have suffered the same affliction with the comfort that I have received from God. As much as I knew I was going to do this, I had difficulty writing about it.

While pregnant, I gladly sat down with my growing miracle baby and tried to write. Within minutes, I realized what the book was to entail and stopped. It couldn't be written without touching on the miscarriages and looking at my strained relationship with God. My relationship with Him had grown distant because of my pain and grief. I was angry with Him. He allowed me to suffer in a way that rocked my faith and trust in Him. This book was going to be a therapeutic journey not only for the reader, but also for its writer.

I decided then that the book could wait, and I would enjoy the pregnancy. I couldn't handle looking back when I was trying to look forward. I was clinging to His promise about this child while beating down fear with His word. The book was not only for His glory, but His way of bringing healing to me. We had some unfinished business, and I wasn't ready to go there yet.

So, here we are three years after my sweet baby Caris Sophia arrived. It's time. I'm not sure what is waiting to be revealed on these pages, but I trust God works all things together for good for those who love Him. *And I do love Him!* To God be the glory and let the Sun of Righteousness arise with healing in His wings.

## Though He Loves Me

Though He loves me
pain still comes
my soul cries today

Days are weathered
by joy and sorrow
life comes to play

Though He loves me
my trials still come
valued more than gold

Though He loves me
my heart breaks
dreams slip away

Though He loves me
seed has died
watered by grief and tears

Though He loves me
death must come
for life to live again

Though He loves me
life gathers ashes
my offering to You

SONG OF THE BARREN

Though He loves me
seasons have sorrow
this world is not my home

*Author Michelle Chudy*
*September 8, 2010*

## A Time to Mourn

*There is a time for everything, and a season for every activity under heaven: a time to be born and a time to die, a time to plant and a time to uproot, a time to kill and a time to heal, a time to tear down and a time to build, a time to weep and a time to laugh, a time to mourn and a time to dance, a time to scatter stones and a time to gather them, a time to embrace and a time to refrain, a time to search and a time to give up, a time to keep and a time to throw away, a time to tear and a time to mend, a time to be silent and a time to speak, a time to love and a time to hate, a time for war and a time for peace. What does the worker gain from his toil? I have seen the burden God has laid on men. He has made everything beautiful in its time. He has also set eternity in the hearts of men; yet they cannot fathom what God has done from beginning to end.*
*Ecclesiastes 3:1-11 (NIV)*

# Chapter 1 - A Shattered Heart

Sometimes you can't appreciate the miracle without walking through the void caused by pain. The angst of the soul makes the gift sweeter and even more precious when finally received. This is easier to say when looking back from the miracle-side of miscarriage.

I don't know if I have the words to describe the times of loss, but I will try. It's necessary to understand where I was in my pain, so you understand my reason to shout for joy. It's the reason for my song and the motivation for this book. It's my deliverance song from barrenness. Not just from barrenness of the womb, but of mind, soul and spirit. My miscarriages created a famine in those areas, too.

I've never experienced pain like that before. Not even when my dad died or from the tragic deaths of our little dogs Tazz and Tate, whom I thought of as my four-legged children. Since the baby was part of me, I felt like part of me was ripped away. And, it was my most vulnerable piece. It was the innocence of hope from the deepest place of me. Fortunately, by the grace of God, I was journaling at the time. All was captured with nothing held back, and it's completely unfiltered. I poured out everything I thought and felt onto paper.

The following are excerpts from my journal which was published in my first book **The Battle of Surrender: One Woman's Journey to Sacrifice**. I'm sharing these with you to give you a glimpse of my journey through miscarriage and the surrounding life events. I hope they help you to better understand me, whom I have become and what has shaped me.

***August 5, 2009*** - *I'm pregnant! I woke up exhausted and emailed my boss this morning that I was going to be working from home. I wrote that I started feeling bad on Friday and it finally caught up with me. After sleeping a couple more hours I got up and started to work. My nausea and fatigue would come and go, and I finally started to get suspicious around noon.*

*My cycle was now five days late. It was in the back of my mind that I could be, but I had started giving up hope. I was even contemplating going back on the pill. Everyone at the office was turning up pregnant except me. There are over ten women pregnant in our department and the last one was a miracle. Little did I know; the Lord already worked His miracle for me.*

*I called my friend in the afternoon, swore her to secrecy and told her what was going on. I hadn't even mentioned it to Mark. She asked if I had taken a pregnancy test. I told her, "Not yet. I'm still working at home in my pajamas." After promising that I would go pick up a test and call her when I knew, I went back to work. Haidyn was home with me so it was going to be a feat to buy it and get it passed her. The kid sees everything especially when you don't want her to.*

*I finally went downstairs to get dressed. I told Haidyn we needed to go out and pick up dinner. She had been asking to buy a toy or something, so I used it as an excuse to stop at Walgreens. While she was distracted looking, I snagged the prenatal vitamins and pregnancy test. I had to laugh since I* was trying to hide the branding and labels from her, as I was carrying them around in the store.

We finally got to the checkout, and I had her stand behind me in the line. I successfully got it on the counter without her seeing, and then the cashier left them for everyone to see without bagging! Successfully cutting her off again and blocking her view, I asked the guy to bag the items quickly. No sooner did he get everything into the bag when one of my coworkers, who I never see outside of work, walks past the register. So much for privacy!

Haidyn and I finally headed home with the stash and dinner. I was trying to wait for the right time to sneak off and take the test. I went into my room and locked the door. Her secret radar detector must have gone off because she was right there banging on the door. I ignored her and waited as the test turned positive. I couldn't believe what I was seeing so I checked the instructions again to make sure I was reading it right. It was positive.

After trying to figure out what to do with the test, I hid it in the closet. I got on my face before the Lord and thanked Him for remembering me. I cried, and I laughed because I was just as irritable as I was happy. Obviously, the hormones had already kicked in because I realized I'm five weeks pregnant.

I decided I would tell Mark by leaving him a note, and his gift of the positive test wrapped up, under his pillow. I waited for him to come home and find it. He got home late and then started messing around the house cleaning. Our housekeeper was coming in the morning, so this is the ritual of the night before she comes to clean. I couldn't take much more of him folding laundry and me staying up late. I was tired and wanted to go to bed! I forgot how tired I was during the first trimester with Haidyn.

As he folded and folded, I grabbed my Bible and headed out to the living room. I sat in the recliner and prayed, Lord, can you make him hurry up, so I can go to bed? A few minutes later, I heard him laughing. Then he said, "You're kidding me, right?" After telling him he took forever to find it, I kissed him and told him he was going to be a daddy again around April 8, 2010. Then I headed off to bed.

**August 9, 2009** - The Church Encounter was this weekend. I had a hard time keeping up because I'm so tired. I was even late for small group on Saturday morning. I told my girls and a handful of coaches, that I was pregnant. I wanted to make sure I had prayer coverage not just for the weekend, but throughout the pregnancy. I asked that they kept the news to themselves until I passed the first trimester. It was funny that when I told a friend, he referred to the baby as "he". I caught the reference immediately and told him that I also believe I'm having a boy...

**August 13, 2009** - What a horrible night! My heart breaks as I write this. I was on the phone with my coworker, talking about all of the crap going on at work. We have just reorganized, and no one can figure out how this new structure is supposed to work. We were deep in conversation, as Haidyn and I walked through the door at home. We dashed in to feed Tate and to let her out, before heading to our hair appointment.

Haidyn ran in before me to get Tater out of the laundry room. The gate was up, but she wasn't inside. Still talking to my friend, I followed Haidyn, and she ran around looking for Tater. She went to Tate's normal hiding spots and back into the living room over by the windows. Haidyn looked outside and started to scream at the top of her lungs.

I already knew what she saw before I looked myself. (It makes me sick to type this.) Little Tater was floating in the pool. Her long hair was spread out on the water. With Haidyn still screaming and me still on the phone, I threw my stuff down, and ran out back to the pool. High heels and all, I went in to get her. She was gone. I held her, sobbing, trying to figure out what happened. Haidyn was hysterical by now. I laid Tate on the chaise and went to Haidyn to try to calm her down. She was running back and forth, yelling she needed to call Daddy.

"I need to call someone!" she yelled. I told her to calm down and go inside. I grabbed the phone, and tried to call Mark, as I went back out to Tate. Haidyn walked back out again far enough to see Tate and started screaming again. She ran back inside. I was having a hard time thinking.

I grabbed a pool towel to cover Tate, so at least Haidyn couldn't see her. I wanted to grab the anointing oil and pray over Tater. I just read about Lazarus being raised from the dead and having the gift of miracles. I would at least ask God to give her back to me. Haidyn kept screaming and running back and forth. She was starting to make me angry because she was completely out of control. I told her to get a grip, and practice self-control. Then the phone rang. It was my coworker.

I tried briefly to explain what happened, but I wanted off the phone. I needed to go pray. I had to call Mark and my stylist Imelda, and I wanted to go pray! My girlfriend was so confused because all she heard was the screaming. My Bluetooth dropped signal when I went outside. She thought we were being attacked.

As Haidyn stood in front of me with her big brown eyes welling with tears, she grabbed my waist and cried, "Why Mommy? Why? Why did she have to die?" My heart ached, and I thought of friends going through a similar loss. How do you answer their questions when you don't understand yourself?

I told her the truth that I didn't know why, and I don't understand it either. I hugged her and asked her to take a deep breath. She begged me to call Daddy. I told her that I was trying to call him, but he wasn't picking up. He was probably on a call at work. I gave her my cell phone and told her to go upstairs and call Aunt Missy.

I was trying to put the pieces together and figure out how this happened. We never let Tate outside by herself. Our housekeeper was there that day, and she must have had the backdoor open while she was cleaning. I'm sure that this wasn't something unusual, but today Tate decided to go out on her own. I'm sure Tate walked down behind the garage, and the housekeeper couldn't see her, assuming she was somewhere in the house. So, she locked the door with Tate outside.

Tater was almost sixteen and in great health, although she was losing her eyesight. She walked into the pool and drowned because no one was there to help her. I still can't figure out why the gate was up in the laundry room without her inside.

Tate had walked into the pool three other times since we've moved here. I've grabbed her by the ponytail to snatch her out of the water twice, and Mark went in with his suit on Easter Sunday to get her. We were always there. Why now?

*Why like this? She was so full of life and love. The thought of her drowning without anyone to help makes me cringe. No matter what precautions we take, we are never in control.*

It was an accident. I kept reminding myself of this. I applied Scripture by guarding my heart from bitterness and taking my thoughts captive by trying not to blame the housekeeper. I learned after losing Tazz how important this was because the strongman of heaviness enveloped me after his death. I let the grief control me and opened a door to oppression. I grieved more over that little dog than any person that has ever died in my life. I had even made a pact long ago with Tazz and Tate that we'd all die together. I renounced it at one of the encounters and broke the soul ties. I'm not sure if you can have a soul tie with animals, but I broke it nonetheless.

With Haidyn distracted by calling my sister, I went outside to pray. I anointed Tate and asked the Lord to restore her life. The little pressure I placed on her side caused blood to pour from her nose. She was gone.

After calling Mark back-to-back, his coworker finally answered his cell. I told him that I needed Mark to get off the phone now, and call home. Mark called within minutes. I told him what happened, and he told his boss he needed to go. He was home in twenty minutes.

Mark got home, and Haidyn clung to him. She started to cry again. After getting her settled down, I told her she could go watch a movie. Mark and I went outside, and he asked if I tried to revive her. I explained I tried to, but she was already gone. He started crying, too. He tried a chest compression *and more blood oozed from her nose. I covered her back up, and we went inside.*

*She was really gone. I had already decided that we would bury her by the bird feeder by the kitchen window. She would be where I could see her, and where God's animals like to play. Mark changed his clothes and started to dig. Like true Texas soil, rock was only two feet below the grass. That poor man spent the next three hours busting through rock that was almost a foot thick. He finally got through and was able to make a space big enough for Tate's bed to slide under the sheet of rock. His hours of digging resulted in bruised hands and his sides worn raw from his jeans rubbing against him. I went upstairs to find something to wrap Tate in to lay her to rest.*

*Tater was such a prissy little dog. Such a foo foo girl, even though she preferred messed up hair. She loved anything soft and fuzzy. I grabbed my poodle blanket. It was satin on one side and a soft coral pile on the other.*

*Haidyn started to throw a fit about me using it and yelled, "No! Mommy, not that. We're supposed to match." Haidyn has a pink poodle blanket, and I had the coral one. It made me instantly angry at her selfish little wants. I snapped at her, "There are more important things in life than matching!"*

*She closed her mouth and followed me downstairs. I went outside and wrapped my precious little dog in my blanket. I wasn't able to bathe her and make her pretty like we did Tazz before his funeral. There wasn't any time to prepare.*

*When I went back out to Mark, he told me that [our cell group leader] Jeff was on his way. He must have called him* when I went inside. Haidyn and I went to Tate's toy basket, picked out two of her favorite toys, and grabbed her treats. We met up outside, and Mark had already brought her around to her grave. When Jeff pulled up, we put her in with her toys and treats, and cried, as Mark prayed and covered her with dirt.

Our little girl was gone, and so was the end of an era in our relationship. Tazz and Tate came into our lives in 1992 and 1993. They were our first kids. We were married for nine years before having Haidyn. I poured my grief of the loss of my dad into the fur of Tazz and Tate, as I hugged and cried over them. They were the keepers of my tears, and often the only ones that saw me the rare times when I cried. They were my constant companions when I was always alone as an Army wife. Through NTC, JTF6, Bosnia, Korea, Gunnery, or whatever training that took Mark away, they were always there. They were great listeners. Tazz loved to sing, and Tate loved to lick. They both knew how to salute and had a repertoire of tricks.

They were both full of love and made everyone laugh. We loved those little dogs as if they were people. If you think of your pet as a dog and keep them outside like an animal, then you don't understand. Ours were angel kisses and an expression of God's love. I'll miss you, Sweet Tater Chudy …my Tater Bug Baby Boogster …I'll miss your sweet little face and fuzzy little feet. Now, I'm left with people.

FIGURE 3: LAST CHRISTMAS TOGETHER
SWEET TATER, HAIDYN (AGE 5) & TAZZ

***August 15, 2009*** - *I woke up today just as tired as I was before I went to bed. I'm not sleeping well. The sight of Tate in the pool is haunting me. Listless, I'm painfully numb and missing her. As much as I want to grieve, I've hidden my sorrow throughout the day from Mark and Haidyn. It's taking my complete focus and self-control to guard my heart and thoughts regarding Tate's death.*

*I decided I would forgive immediately, and not address the accident with the housekeeper. It had to be this way, or it would eat me alive. I told myself that all I would do is cause harm and unnecessary guilt if I said anything. I didn't want to do that. I love and respect the person and know that she is a woman of God.*

*Later in the day, I asked Mark and Haidyn if they wanted to swim. Both declined, and Haidyn said she was mad at the pool because of what happened to Tater. Mark said he kind of felt the same. I have to admit the thought crossed my mind as well.*

*I looked at both of them and said that Satan was trying to ruin a gift that God gave to us. He wanted us to think of the pool as a water of death and tried to ruin Haidyn's baptism memory. [She was baptized in our pool in June.] We decided to swim and not let that happen. I was the first to go in. We all avoided the area where Tate died.*

***August 31, 2009*** - *There wasn't a heartbeat. Surgery is scheduled for 7:00 a.m. on Thursday, so the bleeding will be controlled. I went in expecting the announcement of my baby's due date but received the pronouncement of his death.*

*You could see his little body in the ultrasound, but no heart movement which should be significant at that age. The doctor said he thought it happened last week. I asked if stress could be the cause and he said, "No. The chromosomes just didn't come together."*

*I'm not so sure I believe that. I even remarked a couple of weeks ago that I felt like the enemy was trying to crush him with all of the garbage that was going on...stress was washing over and into me. The little guy was only seven weeks old.*

*Jesus allowed Tate and my baby to die within two weeks of each other. What was the point of allowing me to get pregnant if He knew He was going to let him die? Why both? Why couldn't he have saved Tate if the baby wasn't going to live? August 13th and 31st brought death to me again. As I drove up to the house I felt anger wash over me. Death reigns in this house, and I hate it!*

*I feel like a loose cannon that is loaded, lit, and doesn't know where to aim. As fast as the explosion starts to well up I swallow it back down. Keep your thoughts captive. Guard your heart. I'm numb, mad and dangerously destructive right now. It's easier not to feel. But now that I've had all of that stupid training, I know I can't stuff it too far down. With knowledge comes responsibility and accountability.*

*I need to return the baby bedding. I was so sure it was a boy that I bought a helicopter themed nursery set. It was one of only five left, and I wanted to surprise Mark with it. I called [my sister] Missy to tell her. She and [her husband] Jerry planned a trip just to be here when we told Haidyn. We were going to surprise Haidyn with their visit, take her out to eat and give her the present of her "I'm Going to Be a Big Sister"* t-shirt along with the news. She's been praying for a baby brother or sister since she could talk.

Maybe one day when she is an adult, I'll let her know and show her the picture of her baby brother or sister. At least we'll get to see him in heaven one day. And she'll know that I wanted her to have a baby brother or sister, too. There are some things a parent can't provide to their child without the Lord intervening. This was one of them.

I feel the urge to stuff or starve the void. All of the precautions are senseless now. There is no life to protect other than my own. I feel the impulse to try to meet my own needs by going out and replacing both Tazz and Tate with two bouncing shih tzu puppies. Then I want to destroy my needs by making myself suffer. I want to make Mark suffer because he was such a jerk all weekend.

And as the war rages within, I know that Jesus is Lord and I am not. I will sit here and type out my anger and frustration and let the turbulent frenzied thoughts and emotions fizzle out. So here it is raw and ugly. I will be still and know He is God.

With many questions and no answers, just emptiness is left. It keeps company with my whys. No Tazz or Tate to comfort me and absorb my sorrow. I am now left with God, and I will still praise Him.

For as the heavens are higher than the earth, so are Your ways higher than my ways, and Your thoughts higher than my thoughts. Even when there are no answers, and nothing makes sense, in the good and the bad, God is worthy to be praised. You are the great I AM and I, a vapor, worship You.

And oh, by the way Satan, you stupid devil, I renounce that this house is a house of death. I renounce that my body is the carrier of death. I loose myself from the spirit of death and declare with my mouth it has no ties to me or my household. For we will not die but live to declare the works of the Lord!

**September 1, 2009** - I woke up early today trying to revert to my pre-pregnancy schedule to do my quiet time. I've been so tired the past eight weeks that I've had a hard time getting up. I guess I'm trying to remind my body that it doesn't need sleep anymore even though I still feel pregnant.

I headed to my chair after making my tea. I even switched back to my sweet-n-low since it didn't matter now. Before settling in, I got on my face before God...praying and crying into the carpet...not knowing what I should pray, I let the Holy Spirit pray for me.

I got up and grabbed my "Jesus 90 Days with the One and Only"[1]. The passage was on Mary being great with Child and traveling to Bethlehem for the census. I reflected on how God required the mother of His Son to travel over mountains and valleys to reach His appointed place and time of delivery.

God didn't take it easy on her. You would think He would have supernaturally transported her like He did some of the other people in the Bible. But no, she rode a donkey for miles, while pregnant carrying His Son; a Son, who belonged to the world, which demanded His death, only to give birth in a stable. It was the path God had chosen for her.

I realized as I read that I had started gathering pieces of my life calling them mine like a little child claiming another kid's toys. I was clinging so tightly, I didn't even know it because they had become part of me...Haidyn, Tazz, Tate, my baby, just to name a few. As I sat reading, reality dawned that there is nothing in this life that is really mine. Not even my tears. "You number my wanderings; put my tears into Your bottle; are they not in Your book?" (Psalms 56:8, NKJV). The only thing that is really mine is Jesus.

I headed off to work and spent the morning trying to keep my mind off of things. I'm always behind and there is a ridiculous amount of work to do. It is easy to bury yourself in it.

One of my coworkers came up to give me a hug. He is a brother in Christ and is walking his own painful path with the Lord right now. He is also one of the five at work that I told I was pregnant. When I got home yesterday, I sent a short note to them to let them know that the baby had died.

He asked me, "What are you doing here?" I quipped, "It's better for me to keep my mind off of things." But the more I thought about it throughout the morning, the more I started to wonder, too. What am I doing here? I'm working on things that won't matter for eternity and another crisis was brewing. I decided that after joining Mark for lunch, I was going home.

I drove home to an empty house and wandered around a bit. Every so often, grief welled up from my core, and wailing sobs of grief escaped. I waffled from complete control to sobbing, to praying, to asking God for a miracle. Everything is out of my control, so I gave it to Him. I tried to busy myself but decided to just take a nap instead.

**September 2, 2009** - I worked from home again today. I decided yesterday when I left that I wouldn't go back until after this was all over. They could get their pound of flesh out of me remotely.

I took advantage of the time by working on a mountain of laundry in between fighting with my legal partner who was reviewing my work. Everything is ridiculously unimportant and embedded in inefficiencies. My boss had just mentored me on being more influential than dominating in these situations [...]

Unfortunately, my boss was out for a couple of days, so I was left to my own devices, and I could feel anger simmering. I knew I was becoming volatile. I disengaged and went downstairs to do more laundry. As I dumped the last load on the blanket chest I started to cry angry tears. Looking at the ceiling, I yelled at God for the first time in my life. "Why do You always make me make these decisions? You're the giver of life and death! First Tazz, now the baby. You do it! Why me?"

[Just a few years earlier, Mark and I had to decide to put Tazz down after he slipped a disc which paralyzed him from the neck down. It was like having to kill our son. This heart-wrenching decision was made only after many vet trips, taking him to a chiropractor, acupuncture appointments, herbal treatments and intercessory prayer. He was in so much pain we decided it was best for him. He passed in Mark's arms on January 12, 2007 at the age of fourteen.]

My emotions were churning over whether or not to pursue the D&C. Well-meaning friends were praying that the baby's life be restored and asked that I be certain before I went through with it. There was guilt coming from all directions.

Did I not have enough faith to believe He would give the baby's life back? Would it be an abortion if I had the D&C? Why not wait for it to happen naturally so I would be sure the baby was really dead? I also had in the back of my mind of the possibility of bleeding out if I miscarried naturally. This was a concern stated by the doctor.

*Wailing with grief, I asked God to forgive me for how I approached Him. I told Him I was sorry for being angry with Him. I know He understands, and I resolved to rest in Him.*

**September 3, 2009** - *I've hit bedrock. For the past two years, I've dug deep. Everything covering was removed until the Rock was exposed. My spiritual house is poured on this foundation. I am a living testament that when the floods arose, and the stream vehemently beat on my house, they could not and will not shake it. For my house is founded on the Rock. My God is an awesome God!*

*I woke up at 4:15 a.m. to get ready for the D&C. I had to be there by 6:00 a.m. As I showered, and let the water wash away my remaining tears, they were different this time. They were ones of agreement and submission that only come with the peace of God.*

*There was no wailing grief this time, just a cleansing stream coming from a quiet spirit. I still don't understand, but I know He has plans to prosper me and not harm me. His Word promises me this.*

*I drove myself to the hospital and walked the path that the Lord had chosen for me before time was written. I went alone, since Mark had to get Haidyn on the bus. He met me right before the procedure.*

*As I lay in the hospital bed answering all of the questions, both medical and social, I told the staff I don't need margaritas (which they jokingly offered) or anything else other than God.*

*When asked by the anesthetist if I had any vices...alcohol, smoking, drugs, caffeine, etc., I told him no. My only vice was God. After thinking on that a little longer, sugar did come to mind, so I had to fess up. I'm sure that will be the next thing* to go when God gets the chisel out again. I laugh because I ate seven cookies today. I can't blame the baby for this weight gain.

I spoke to the doctor prior to surgery and he reassured me the heartbeat stopped and the baby had passed at seven weeks. I knew in my spirit that this was the truth of Jesus. I would have been nine weeks pregnant today.

I had prayed before walking in. I asked Jesus to minimize the pain, if possible. He answered that and more. The IV stick was barely felt due to a topical, the surgery took less time than planned and was without complications, and I even came out of anesthesia quickly.

The anesthesia was a concern for me because the three times I've been under before, I've had a hard time coming out of it. The Lord even blessed me with Mark at my side and an angel of a nurse on the other. She was comforting and sweet and had Kleenex in hand to catch the tears Mark and I shed.

The nurse said that there was significant blood loss and it was wise to have had the D&C. This made me feel even better. I knew that if I let things happen naturally there was a chance of bleeding out because the doctor had voiced concern over the size of the placenta. When I talked to Missy later today she told me that I lost more blood than she did from her hysterectomy. The Lord gave me witnesses to confirm my decision was the right one.

Mark and I came home and napped until noon. The pain has been managed by over-the-counter medicine instead of the prescribed narcotic. I feel the heaviness in my womb but know it's only from the effects of this world. God will replace it with healing and life if He so chooses. "The righteous cry out, and the Lord hears, and delivers them out of all their troubles. The Lord is near to those who have a broken heart and saves such as have a contrite spirit. Many are the afflictions of the righteous, but the Lord delivers him out of them all" (Psalms 34:17-19, NKJV). This came from the passage the Holy Spirit gave me this morning. I'm in a good place.

As Mark went to pick up Haidyn at the bus stop, I thought I'd take the time to stay up and write. I wanted to take advantage of the time I had by myself. As I got up from my desk to walk to the bathroom, I felt woozy and the need to lie down. Heeding the signs of my body I went to the couch.

As I flipped through the channels intending to watch "I Love Lucy", I felt the prompting to go to God TV. The Lord put me on the couch to watch a teaching from Derek Prince. It was the first and only time I had seen his broadcast available on Sky Angel since we got it a year ago. Derek was teaching part two of "Founded on the Rock"[2] series. It was God ordained that I watch it.

---

> But why do you call Me 'Lord, Lord,' and do not do the things which I say? Whoever comes to Me, and hears My sayings and does them, I will show you whom he is like: he is like a man building a house, who dug deep and laid the foundation on the rock. And when the flood arose, the stream beat vehemently against that house, and could not shake it, for it was founded on the rock.
> Luke 6: 46-48 (NKJV)

---

*Through Derek's opening statements, Jesus showed me that I've hit bedrock. Derek was teaching on the parable of the builder from Luke 6. He pointed out that there is a significant difference in the gospel of Luke. Luke is the only one that mentions that it took deep digging to get to the rock.*

*Derek pointed out that this may be the removal of many worldly things or false beliefs to expose Jesus in your life. Jesus showed me that this is exactly what I've been doing for the past two years...we have dug deep, and I'm standing on the Rock.*

*During this past month, the rain of death and grief came crashing in, pain of confusion and anger beat on my door, while stress and irritability tried to flood me. And as I've sat weeping since August 13th, I leaned on the knowledge and words of my Savior.*

*As mad as it made me that I couldn't run off with my old bad behaviors, I did what the Lord taught me. I took my thoughts captive, I guarded my heart, and I pled with my God as the saints blanketed me in prayer. I worked through the pain of not understanding by taking Job's stance of humility that my God is bigger than me and His ways are higher. I rested in Him.*

*Jesus means what He says, and He can be trusted. His grace is sufficient, and He never leaves nor forsakes. When I walked through the valley of the shadow of death, He was with me and often carried me. His peace does pass understanding because I still don't understand, but I do have His peace. I now understand what this verse truly means. It's no longer just a Vacation Bible School song.*

*He is a mighty God and an awesome God. He is my Rock and my salvation. This world is temporal, and it will pass* away. But the Lord and His righteousness are for eternity. And when I reach eternity, my questions will be answered, and I will know that He only permitted me to suffer for His greater glory. My baby is with His creator playing with his puppies Tazz and Tate, while Grandma Anna and Grandpas John and Joe are waiting to baby sit. I praise Him and serve Him alone.

**September 4, 2009** - I woke up feeling okay even after having a crappy night's sleep. You would think that I would at least be granted a decent night's sleep after all of this. I lay there for quite some time not able to sleep, and then tossed and turned all night. Mark was wrestling around, too. My hormones must be flushing. I go from being fine to sad and then weepy.

There was very little pain this morning, and I thanked God for that. As I was thinking over the week's events, I tried to keep the bitterness from creeping in. There were a lot of unnecessary pain points along the way.

The surgical center called me over fifteen times trying to get information, and most of the calls were concerning collection of payment. They failed to notice, I had already signed a document on Monday that gave them permission to charge the extra costs to my insurance card.

One of the nurses I spoke to was very rude. Then there was a string of calls after 3:30 p.m. Tuesday trying to get me to have the procedure the next day. No explanation, just multiple messages. I didn't get the messages until Wednesday morning, but then noticed the last one said to disregard the request. We were still on for Thursday morning at 7:00 a.m. While I was still trying to process the death of my child, and use what little time I was given, I'm sure they were *trying to accommodate someone's schedule, so they could leave early for the long weekend.*

*Here are some random thoughts that came to mind during this heartbreaking experience. If you are a healthcare professional, don't forget the place of ministry you have been given. What may be a daily work experience for you, is not for the patient. Don't ever forget the value of life and your impact on it. Your one moment of kindness, or rudeness, may be the last thing received before receiving a medical death sentence. If you've lost touch with the patient's reality, then get another job. Your salt has lost its flavor. And never forget that medicine is an instrument of God. He is the divine Healer and all things are possible through Him. Don't assume His role and overstep your rights that He gave you.*

*Don't judge a person by religious affiliation. Going to the same church doesn't make your beliefs the same. Everyone has their own walk with God and some are further along than others. Any mixture with the world dilutes faith, and their fruit and words will show what's in their heart.*

*Having gone through the experience of a miscarriage I realize that people really don't know how to minister to someone in this situation. Do you call, bring food, and acknowledge the loss? Yes!!! Make the effort! I will tell you every prayer, visit, call, and email were heartfelt and treasured. My precious friends Audrey and Sonia even brought a meal. It was greatly appreciated. Although this baby never made it into the world, he was fearfully and wonderfully made. His death was real. His life was a response to things hoped for and a heart's desire. His life was cherished, and it will be missed and grieved.*

*So, make the call, and let the person decide if they want to talk. If they don't pick up, leave a message. It makes a* difference knowing you have someone that cares if you need to reach out. They will never know how much you cared unless you let them know. Silence doesn't erase the grief and pain.

**September 6, 2009** - I spent most of today angry, hateful and not so motivated to move past it. I'm also exhausted. I couldn't sleep last night again. I prowled around until 2:00 a.m. and then flopped around in bed until 3:30 a.m. I was so emotional, I wanted to weep.

I lay beside Mark trying to cry without waking him but wanting to be close. He doesn't know how much I struggle each night of wanting to be near him, but afraid to draw close. I stayed long enough to wet his shoulder then got up again. I grabbed the Kleenexes and crawled back to my side of the bed, where I drew into myself.

The healing Scriptures were still playing. "Jesus, help me," was all I could muster, and I lay there mad because I couldn't sleep. I also had in the back of my mind that the healing Scriptures were on when the baby died. I've been listening to it nightly for a couple of weeks.

The alarm went off around 8:00 a.m. so I could get ready for church. Haidyn was already up. I could hear her moving around upstairs. She was trying to act like she wasn't awake and didn't answer when I called for her. I yelled up the staircase, "I know you're awake. Come down."

She's been distant toward me since Thursday. My little girl is very discerning, and I know she knows there is more going on than me having blood work done. She has a passive aggressive way of making her anger known. She likes to ice me out; like mother like daughter.

We grabbed our breakfast and went outside to watch the birds as we ate. She was sharing her secrets, and I had to promise not to tell Daddy. I sat there amazed at how beautifully individual she is and how fast she is growing up. So many big emotions and understandings reside in that precious little eight-year-old body. We went inside to do some space planning and measuring that was a result of my late-night internet surfing. Mark finally woke up as we finished measuring the upstairs.

I had already laid out her clothes for church and gave her instructions to get ready. As I went around her room, I noticed she had stuffed things under the bed, in the closet and under the dresser, instead of putting them away. Of course, she learned this from one of her friends during a play date.

In a matter of seconds, I got angry and short-tempered with her. After telling her she had too many things and that she didn't appreciate any of them, I threatened to give everything to someone who cared. This made her immediately start the, "No Mommy, no! I promise I'll stop!" This is whining that never results in changed behavior. It made me even angrier. I left the room in a huff as Mark went to her rescue. Of course, he acts like the hero when he's the one that is not making her cry.

I noticed the time and told him that we probably wouldn't make it to church. He insisted that we go, so I went downstairs to rush so we would get there on time. After I hurried, he was still messing around. He wasn't even close to shaving and was still in his boxers. Now he was going to make us late and that made me start to seethe.

I felt the mental war begin as thoughts flooded in of all of his faults. He's always the last to get up. Then the thought turned to because he is always sleeping. Before I could stop myself, I said something about him making us late. This of course set him off and we began arguing.

As we hurled words back and forth, he started accusing me of various things. All I could think about was how he had no clue of my emotional turmoil and the toll this experience was taking on my hormones, body and emotions.

As hardness enveloped me, I looked at him and facetiously thanked him for his support. I then told him the only thing I could count on him for was not being there for me. They were words that should never have been spoken. I didn't even mean them.

After he stormed out of the bathroom, everything in me wanted to be someplace far away from him. I definitely didn't want to go to church with him. I made myself finish getting ready and resolved that I would go. I knew Satan was there feeding my emotional inferno. It was trying to consume me and everyone in its path.

We got into the truck to leave knowing that service had already started. I didn't have a word to say. Detachment was in full force. I knew I had to guard my heart and to make sure the gates were up. The anger was like trying to rein in wild horses.

Praise and worship was in full swing by the time we made it to church. We stood waiting for the usher to let us in after the song was over. I made a point to get behind Mark, so he could find us seats. It was the least he could do since he made us late.

As we walked to the pew, I noticed the communion tables. That was just great! I sat through the service angry while eyeing the communion. I had three choices: I could pass on the communion and go home with the anger; I could stay *angry and take communion which would make me unworthy and bring damnation on myself; or I could give the anger to Jesus, ask forgiveness and be fit to participate. I also knew I needed the healing that communion provides, and it wouldn't be wise to pass. I had sixty minutes to decide, and I used almost every minute to settle things with Jesus. At the last moment, I asked Mark to forgive me, too.*

*We went home and even though my sins were forgiven, my hormones were still a train wreck. The pregnancy hormones must be flushing. I felt physically and emotionally depleted. I started to get irritable about all of the unfinished projects around the house to include writing in this journal. Nothing ever gets finished. There is never enough time. Fed up with everything, I decided I would go take a nap. I lay there, struggling to sleep, not understanding anything about why this had to happen. I had to stop picking up these thoughts. I finally fell asleep and took a much-needed, two-hour nap.*

*Mark and Haidyn got ready to go to church for evening service. I decided to stay back. I had every intention of writing and catching up on my entries. However, I spent most of the time reading my testimony and remembering. How soon we forget the great things God has done for us and taught us. It was also a reminder that I needed to work out my salvation with fear and trembling, as I press on for the prize. All I know is, recently each day is a struggle to remember and claim the*

*Word of God. It's a choice that I need to make each moment of the day. This has been a tough lesson.*

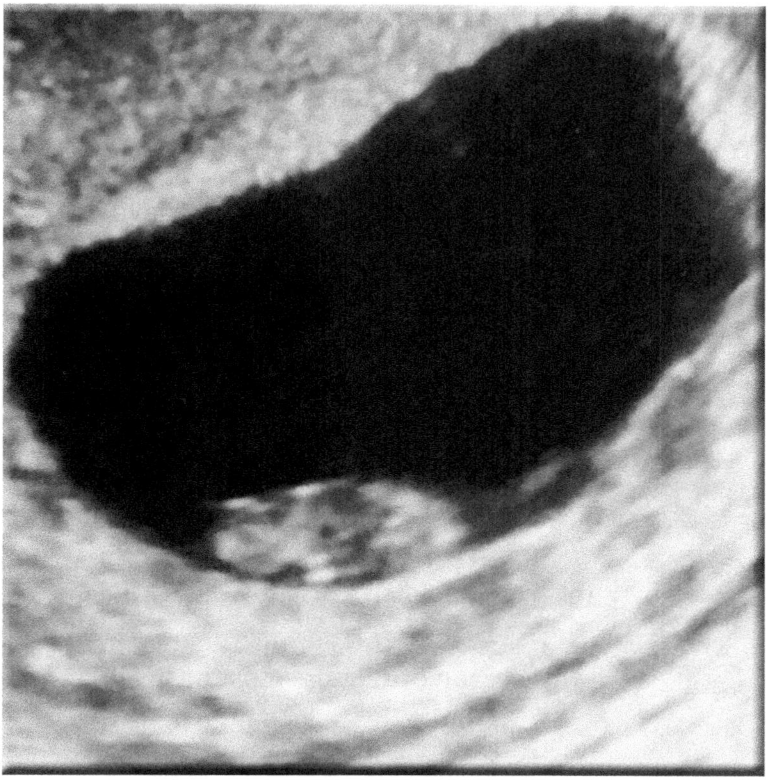

FIGURE 4: JOHN MARK CHUDY
HEAVEN BORN - AUGUST 31, 2009

## Michelle Renée Chudy

### Too Tired to Breathe

When life is heavy, too tired to breathe
sorrow lines my day
Behind each smile sadness hides
tears find their way

Nowhere to hide, nowhere to grieve
my life marches on
I swaddle feelings with stillborn dreams
I cradle up my pain

When death goes unnoticed, no one sees
no one understands
How do you explain a love for loss
that was never lived?

With head bowed as sighs come softly
I suffer labor pain
This season of sadness must be lived
but only for its days

I come to Jesus with my burden
that was birthed to me
How precious are my tears to Him
I cry for help today

I fall before the altar of grace
I lay my burden down
As torrents of tears flood my face
exchange them for a crown

When life is heavy, too tired to breathe
Jesus draws me near

## Song of the Barren

My children that are heaven born
are bathed with my tears

One day soon I'll see their faces
then I'll understand
Sometimes glory requires a price
only paid for with my tears

*Author Michelle Chudy*
*September 12, 2010*

## Chapter 2 - Fool Me Twice

*As the heavens are higher than the earth,
so are My ways higher than your ways
and My thoughts than your thoughts.
Isaiah 55:9 (NIV)*

**August 27, 2010** - I knew it! I was starting to get suspicious about a week ago. I'm pregnant! I'm almost five weeks, and the baby is due May 1st. I must have gotten pregnant right after the Youth Encounter.

Over the past week even though I think I knew, I felt a cloak of denial wrap around me. Emotionally I don't believe I was ready to hope again. I told Jesus that I was sorry, but I still think I have hurt feelings over the miscarriage. I had so much faith the last pregnancy, but it obviously didn't align with His will. Understanding was never achieved over the loss of the last baby, only acceptance of what I couldn't change. I was starting to fall into the mindset of nothingness. I didn't want to hope or to yearn, while thinking His will was going to happen, regardless of my wants and desires.

I stopped at the store on the way home debating about buying the pregnancy test. The Lord brought to remembrance the dream I had almost two years ago. It was of Mark, Haidyn, me and our son. Haidyn was a beautiful, petite young *adult walking in with her daddy. I came in behind walking with our son. He was beautiful with black hair and blue eyes. He was a pre-teen. I knew it wasn't a dream of heavenly reunion because Haidyn was mad at me in the dream. That's why she was clinging to Mark. She's done that since she was a baby. When she's mad at one of us, she'll cling to the other, and act like you don't exist. I asked Jesus if this baby was the boy in my dream. I didn't hear Him answer but felt like I at least needed to find out for sure. I never want to act under a spirit of denial again.*

*I know that trusting Him will be the test of this pregnancy. I choose to trust that God is protecting this child, and I will not fear the what ifs. God chose to knit this child together and place him in my womb. He has numbered his days and placed a great calling on his life. He will be mighty in the kingdom. This is a season of change in our home and the breeze indicates the winds of great things to come. I place my hope and trust in Jesus alone, for me and my child.*

**September 5, 2010** - *I'm not sure what is going on. I'm six weeks pregnant today and started bleeding last night with some minor cramping today. I don't go to the doctor until the twentieth. I went online and found it could be normal, or the early signs of a miscarriage. Emotionally, I'm cautious because I don't know what to expect of Him this time. Is there such a thing as guarded hope? The only thing I can do is leave it in His hands because it's out of my control. I pray that my assigned portion in this area of life was met last year, and that I don't have to walk the path again.*

**September 7, 2010** - *We went to the doctor this morning. They confirmed the miscarriage. My hope was as faint going in, as faint as the line on the pregnancy test, when the nurse attempted to confirm the pregnancy. My pregnancy symptoms are quickly fading away. An ultrasound was done* just to make sure, and it looked like the miscarriage took care of itself. No D&C this time, thank God.

It hurts differently this time. It's not a bottomless sorrow, but more of a dull ache, emotionally and physically. I really don't understand why I am supposed to go through this again. Maybe it was for Mark and me to come together and grieve over the loss of both babies. We didn't do so well the last time.

God's will is sometimes strange and lonely. I struggle with why He would let me get pregnant knowing the baby would die. What is the point? What did I not learn from the last time? I've told Him I'm content with Haidyn, if His will is for me to only have one child. I've asked Him to reconcile my desires to His. I've laid mine down. In the midst of it all, I know He is here. Sometimes I wish He would answer my questions. Exactly one year later I'm back to a familiar grief. I'm not angry this time, just sad and empty. I'm trying to praise Him, but my heart is flat. Maybe it's time to just be still and know that He is God, and I am not.

**September 17, 2010** - I am depleted. I feel like I'm running on fumes with nothing left to give. Surely this isn't the meaning of being at the end of yourself? I wake up exhausted after going to bed exhausted. It feels like my blood was let overnight. My dreams are peppered with things that aren't pleasant. They're nothing scary now, but something with enough of an irritant to rob me of peace while sleeping.

I know that my iron is off due to the blood loss from the miscarriages. I have most of the symptoms of iron deficiency, all but the desire to eat dirt, paint and ice. So far, we're good on that one, thank God. I guess I'll know I'm in bad shape when I start chewing on the walls.

*In the middle of my quiet time Mark called. He wanted to share that he had spoken with Haidyn's teacher. During recess yesterday, Haidyn was on the swings playing by herself which is unlike her. One of Haidyn's friends told the teacher that she was really sad. When the teacher went over to her, Haidyn said she is just missing her mom. I know she is because I can see it when she's at the house. There isn't enough time in the morning and evening, and there isn't anything left when we're together. Life keeps rolling along, and I feel like I'm under its tires.*

*I cried out to Abba today to ask Him to remember us. This is not what we've prayed for and it's not what I desire. Everywhere I turn, I see no opportunity for exit. I am in the waiting place that is so accurately described in "Oh, the Places You'll Go"*[3]*. I'm so ready to escape to find the bright places where the boom bands are playing.*

**September 21, 2010** - *I left for work this morning trying to figure out how I can quit my life. I concluded that at this point, it's not an option. I'd like to take a nap for about six weeks with the hope of waking up with energy. The irony is I want to be at home but am forced into life instead. I can't wait to get the full story from Jesus on what He is working behind the scenes.*

*I'm tired of the ugliness of life that tries to dwell in our home. It was tumultuous in the house before we left this morning. When I'm tired, I normally don't have the patience to keep my mouth shut. Mark was badgering Haidyn over her homework, and her tone was becoming disrespectful. He was provoking her. It's one thing to know you need to fix a problem when you're looking back and feeling remorseful. But when you're in the heat of bad behavior, it tends to breed companions. I didn't fare so well in demonstrating the godly wife behaviors. I managed to keep some snide remarks back* but wasn't successful with all. I know I can only change me, but sometimes I wish God would focus on others for a while.

When I got to work, I was feeling pretty dejected. Looking for parking at the building is enough to make you think that you've lost favor. I ended up outside in the Visitor's Lobby and the forecast is for rain. When I walked to my desk, everyone was smiling when I passed them and actually made eye contact. There was a package on my chair with a nice thank you note from the person I loaned my Beth Moore CDs. She thanked me for encouraging her and noted our relationship is for an eternity. As soon as I sat down, one of my coworkers came by with gifts for being on the team. She found out about the miscarriage yesterday and was very sweet. I had a chance to testify of what God is doing in my life. Then when I went to the cafeteria for my morning tea, one of my favorite workers was there. I could tell she was feeling down. Her family is going through a rough time with various illnesses and a recent diagnosis of cancer. I prayed with her for her peace and strength. Even though I want to hide in my house and hibernate, Jesus is showing me that I still have work to do in His field. He is using me in spite of myself.

It's not about my strength, but His. I actually had a word from Him on Saturday when I was doing my quiet time. During my prayers He said, "You will serve me as you are. You will serve me the way I made you. My Word is in you. It is enough." Knowing that I'll never have enough in my own right, I'm reassured that it's His Word, that it is sufficient…

## Chapter 3 - Love Has a Name

The rebound time after the last miscarriage seemed quick, maybe too quick. For those who didn't know I was pregnant, they had no idea. I went back to work acting like all was well, even though I was a mess. A week after the second miscarriage, I went to an offsite meeting for work and was assigned a project that marketed a baby onesie. My boss was one of the few people in the know of the miscarriage and offered to give the assignment to someone else. I was adamant and nonchalant about keeping the project. I was getting good at keeping the stiff upper lip. I'd been practicing it for a year.

One of the hardest things while playing this part happened on August 31, 2009, the day I found out the first baby died. The date was to be one of celebration. The doctor's appointment was set to check for the heartbeat and determine my due date. My then best friend was also pregnant and ready to deliver her second child. Her induction was scheduled that same day. We thought it was beautiful for us to share the day for celebration, since both babies were gifts and a result of our prayers. But, our celebratory paths split as the day wore on. By the time I got home from the appointment with the decree of the death of my child, she had delivered her healthy, beautiful baby girl.

Still reeling from my news, I made myself call to congratulate her. She was still in the hospital. I listened to every detail and asked her to share more. I tried to keep her talking, so I wouldn't have to; however, she was my best friend. She asked about my appointment. I was evasive with my answer and told her it was her day and to keep talking. I would share later. I didn't want my pain to overshadow her joy.

So, I ordered her roses and the personalized door sash with her baby girl's name. I went shopping that weekend to buy baby items for the gift basket. Mark, Haidyn and I made the perfunctory visit when they got home. What kind of friend would I be if I punished her for living out my dream?

After round two of miscarriage, I made it a point to move on and not to think. I was working in corporate chaos and also in the throes of publishing *The Battle of Surrender*. I had deadlines and meetings to distract my thoughts.

A few months later, I was at work walking back to my office, when I ran into my best friend in the hall. She wanted to talk to me about something. She was reading *Heaven is For Real*[4] and had something she wanted to share. Enthralled by the book, she thought I would be blessed by reading it. She gently mentioned there is a chapter in the book that talks about miscarriage. She thought I would be encouraged by reading it.

My friend then apologized for not being there for me after the first miscarriage. She mentioned being so overwhelmed with work, and a newborn, she didn't realize how much I was hurting. With tears in her eyes that brought tears to mine, she said, "In the book there is a miscarried baby who is very alive in heaven but has no name. The baby doesn't have a name because her mom didn't give her one when she died." I didn't know what to say. The conversation was getting to be too much for a hallway chat. I could feel the tears starting to well up. I hugged her and said thanks, so I could quickly move along before the pain resurfaced in a downpour of tears.

By that stage in our friendship, I regarded these conversations as a message from the Lord via my friend. I knew the Lord used her to help me in ways I wouldn't or couldn't help myself. I went out and bought the book.

Over the weekend, I sat by my pool and sobbed as I read the book. It made me rethink of how I saw my two miscarriages...my babies. They were no longer dead to me, or a dehumanized situation labeled with the miscarriage term, but living eternal children waiting for me in heaven. I was a mother of *three* children, not just one. I decided I was not going to have nameless kids running around heaven. So, I gave them each a name based on their gender, which I knew, and sensed in my spirit. My son is John Mark and his little sister is Abigail Annalise.

## Chapter 4 - Sissy Love...Haidyn's Letter

When I first found out that my mom lost the babies, I was upset. I guess I was in shock. I remember the day that my mom told me about the miscarriages. I was confused. I remember thinking why would God allow this to happen to a poor innocent baby?

I had always wanted a little sibling and knowing that I could have had two of them just broke my heart. It's like finally holding onto the thing you had wanted most and then watching it get ripped out of your grasp. It's something that you push to the back of your mind and hope that you never have to deal with. I put those feelings away because it wasn't something to talk about. Your friends don't get it. No one really gets it unless they have gone through it themselves.

I don't really think about them much, but it's painful when I do. I try to keep it locked away because it just brings back all of those memories. You think of the relationships that could have been and now aren't. You think of the lives they could've lived and the dreams they could have achieved. It's not a fond memory, but it's something you learn to deal with. Sometimes I imagine how crazy my family would be with two other kids, but it's hard to even think about.

People who go through miscarriages all have different stories and experiences. It's hard to think about it sometimes, but it is something that needs to be dealt with. It's a difficult subject, but once you finally talk about it there *is healing. It's reassuring to know that you will see the sweet babies again in heaven.*

*~ **Haidyn Elise**, Age 15*

MICHELLE RENÉE CHUDY

## *Well of Barrenness*

I walked a path
I know so well
& kneeled to take a drink

My reflection gazed
as I looked at me
a barrenness dry and deep

I cupped my hands
and drank the dust
of my dry and empty well

Always thirsty
for something more
this barrenness cannot fill

Today I choose
a different path
and walk in valleys still

Pastures green
I thirst no more
I've found a Living Well

*Author Michelle Chudy*
*June 9, 2009*

## Chapter 5 - The Place Between

There is a place between hope and hopelessness. It's marked by time, but it is not the waiting place as so aptly described by our beloved Dr. Seuss. It is more like a desert; vast, dry, and seemingly never ending. I found myself walking that terrain soon after the second miscarriage. It goes on and on, until the reality of it sucks you dry. It's the place where you see life based on your reality, but it's not necessarily your truth. Dreams die of thirst there.

As time moved on, my heart didn't, and I found it hardening toward certain things. It was almost a side effect necessary for survival, in order to cope with inconsiderate, well-meaning people, even the self-proclaiming Christian ones. Grief made them uncomfortable, let alone talking about a death that wasn't real to them. There was nowhere to release the pain because no one cared to listen. Life-in-utero is ambiguous for some and my two hadn't passed the threshold of this world to merit attention. *Life* was too busy. *Stop moping and move on! Give it to the Lord and keep going!* Grieving didn't seem permitted, so my heart got tough again. And there's something about returning baby items that you purchased with joy, which mocks your heart's desires, and stiffens your emotions.

Family didn't understand why I wouldn't raise my hand for prayer to receive another baby, when it was offered by the guest speaker at the Mother's Day banquet. What do you say to the nail tech or grocery store clerk who chastises you for only having one child, exclaiming you should have more than one? *One is no good! You should have two!* Or the friend who jokingly says you're not a real mom, until you have more than one child? Should I tell them my sob story of how I wanted more children, but that they died in my womb?

And then there is the lonely little girl, who really wants a baby brother or sister. She prayed every night waiting to see if God was listening. She then started asking about foster care and adoption when it seemed like He wasn't. *Would you be willing? Why not Mommy? Please Mommy?* I wondered if I was willing, and if I would be able to love a foster or adopted child. Not that there is anything wrong with fostering or adopting. I feared that I wouldn't. Willing meant that I would have to open my heart up again. It was still weeping inside of its hardened walls.

To cope, my world became defined by what I permitted myself to think and feel. God's Word seemed to have less power because it didn't save my babies. My faith was dull or would only come in spurts because it was choked by stifled grief. The weed of bitterness had also found its way into my garden. My living "baby" was now a very mature tween. Children were no longer cute and desirable. I started to revert and see them as I did before I got pregnant with Haidyn. I didn't like them then, especially, the undisciplined disrespectful ones. Haidyn was the only one I wholeheartedly loved, along with my new fur babies Zach and Zoey.

Hopelessness flattened any thought that whispered for another baby. I resigned to keep things as they were. If even a couple of days late for my period, I found myself begging God not to be pregnant. *Not this time. Not yet*, I would pray.

It would irritate me if anyone else mentioned pregnancy to me. Even driving by the baby specialty stores would make me turn my head and look the other way. I avoided baby showers and giving baby gifts. Isn't it strange how a dream so desired can turn into an aversion that closely resembles resentment or vehement dislike? Unknowingly, I had pitched my tent in the land of barrenness. Content or not, it was where I intended to stay.

## A Time to Believe

> And without faith it is impossible to please God, because anyone who comes to Him must believe that He exists and that He rewards those who earnestly seek Him. Hebrews 11:6 (NIV)

> For all of the promises of God in Him are Yes, and in Him Amen, to the glory of God through us.
> 1 Corinthians 1:20 (NKJV)

## Chapter 6 - Cramps and Cravings

*For the Lord will comfort Zion, He will comfort all her waste places; He will make her wilderness like Eden, And her desert like the garden of the Lord; Joy and gladness will be found in it, Thanksgiving and the voice of melody.*
*Isaiah 51:3 (NKJV)*

Denial has a way of confounding the wise, but God's plan has a way of mocking Satan's lies. Three years later, I'm seven months into a new job that I relocated across the country to accept. I wasn't looking for work when the recruiter reached out to me. I had no desire to leave my life in Texas. Regardless, I was ready for a change and accepted the offer after much prayer. It was a fresh start and a new chapter. The new position and move brought much needed stress relief, even though it was bittersweet leaving my church, family and beloved Texas behind. My life, and all of its pieces and parts, became manageable after we moved.

In the fall, only months after starting my new job, I flew to San Francisco for business to attend a conference. It was a quick trip, but a long flight. On the way there, a fellow passenger coughed the entire time. From the moment I heard the first cough, I dreaded flu exposure. Sure enough, I was sick by the weekend I returned home. The doctor wasn't convinced it was the flu because of how quickly it passed, but all of the symptoms matched. He thought it was some kind of flu-like virus.

Random symptoms kept on through Christmas, where I just felt run down. Then add hot flashes, weight gain and not sleeping well. I was convinced that I was starting menopause. Shortly after my trip to San Francisco, we traveled west for a family event. While on the trip to Nebraska, I had a lengthy conversation with my sister-in-law about bio-identical hormone therapy. She had just gone through a year of menopausal hell and had great results from the therapy. I was sold! I called and set an appointment with my new OBGYN to discuss hormone supplements. The appointment was two weeks away.

I was forty-four and my cycle was starting to get unpredictable. I thought my only ovary was getting tired and punking out after twenty-one years of working solo. At one point, the cramping was really bad. I sat down, while pulling in my knees, leaned over and prayed for my period to start, so the misery would end. Thank God for that unanswered prayer!

When sharing my "issues" with my coworker, who is the same age as me, she laughed and asked, "Are you sure you're not pregnant?" No doubt I glared at her. But over the weekend I started to wonder. I was really craving orange juice. That one symptom alone weaved its way through my adamant denial of not being pregnant and made me suspicious.

When I was pregnant with Haidyn, it was the one item I craved over everything else. It also caused me to gain thirteen pounds in the first trimester. The doctor was convinced I was eating junk food and didn't really believe that I was eating healthy. In fact, after I found out I was pregnant; I gave up my wicked junk food ways of soda, Funyuns and strawberries for lunch. It was all natural, real food, fruits and vegetables for me and the baby. After much convincing, the doctor suspected gestational diabetes and tested me early. I flunked. I also loved the sugary coke drink that made most women puke. Sadly, no more orange juice for me from that point forward. The juice was turning into sugar in my system and making my glucose spike, which contributed to the extra pounds.

Fast forward to twelve years later...After church that following Sunday, I *really* wanted orange juice. I asked Mark to stop at the store on the way home to source my craving. With OJ in the cart, I also snuck-purchased a pregnancy test. My coworker's words kept dancing around in the back of my mind. It was better to know than to not.

I had more concerns other than miscarriage. My system wasn't clean. I wasn't taking vitamins and had taken allergy medicine daily for months. It was the kind you shouldn't take while pregnant because of unknown effects, or possible birth defects. To prepare for Haidyn, I took six months to detox my body and supplemented with prenatal vitamins prior to trying to conceive. At this point, I hadn't made any efforts to eat clean or eliminate medications, but at least I was decaffeinated thanks to a fast at the beginning of the year.

We finally made it home with the juice and my hidden purchase. I waited for everyone to settle in for their Sunday afternoon nap and then took the test in private. I was hesitant. I carefully read and reread the instructions, then took the test, and waited. It was positive!

As I stared at the stick, I had a sinking feeling and hint of joy at the same time. I didn't know what to think. It was surreal. There was no doubt it was a positive result. The color was dark, and the symbol clearly indicated pregnant. *Now what? Who should I tell? Anyone?* I didn't want anyone to know. *What if it's positive, but the baby is dead like the last time?* I stopped taking the allergy medicine immediately.

I debated about not telling Mark and just going to the doctor by myself. That way, if the test was wrong or something happened, no one would be hurt. I decided that at least Mark should know. It wasn't right to keep it from him. The baby was as much his as mine.

I waited for him to get up from his nap to show him the results. He was happy and said it was an answer to his prayer. That surprised me. I didn't know he was still praying for a baby. I assumed he gave up on another child and moved on like I did. We both agreed that we wouldn't tell Haidyn or anyone else about this baby until after the first trimester. The doctor's appointment was the next hurdle to clear.

The next morning, the first thing I did when I got to my office was to call the doctor. After explaining my history to the nurse, she worked quickly to get me in as soon as possible. My appointment was scheduled for the following morning. They would do an ultrasound. I was impressed and relieved that it was scheduled so soon, but twenty-four hours felt like an eternity.

## Chapter 7 - Blessed Assurance

*However, as it is written: "No eye has seen, no ear has heard, no mind had conceived what God has prepared for those who love Him."*
*1 Corinthians 2:9 (NIV)*

Uneasy and blissfully numb would be a great description of how I arrived at the doctor's appointment that morning. In order to divert my thoughts, my strategy to overcome the worry and fear was through distraction. By the time I walked through the hospital door and down the hall to the doctor's office suite, déjà vu tried to creep its nasty self into my thoughts and emotions. The fact that Mark was with me, helped stop me from going down memory lane. It also helped that I'd never been to this doctor or location. I was still new to town and hadn't yet established the patient-doctor relationship. This was my first visit.

I'm not sure how Mark felt or what he was thinking. I didn't want to ask if he was afraid of receiving bad news again. Small talk with Mark, my Blackberry and iPhone, along with nonsensical programs on the waiting room TV, kept my thoughts entertained until they called us back for the appointment.

Amazed by the kindness and efficiency of the nursing staff, it was now my turn. I quickly got into my room. My apprehension lifted somewhat because the staff was so cheerful. I wasn't sure what I had signed up for with this doctor, since I was initially looking for menopause treatment. I picked her from a website profile. There wasn't any thought of obstetric needs. This negated the need to investigate service philosophy or patient rapport. Thank God, the doctor was the perfect match for me. She was confident, competent, down-to-earth and easy to talk to. She was genuine and really seemed to care.

It's funny how the Lord works to comfort you because we also discovered a family tie between us. She was part of a great family whom we knew from our home church while living in Elizabethtown, Kentucky. They are a very godly family. This relaxed me even more because I knew that faith and miracles would probably not be foreign to her.

As I lay on the table, it seemed like it took forever to get the ultrasound ready. Because of my history, they decided to do a vaginal ultrasound since it gives a more accurate reading. Looking back, it almost seems funny because I started talking a lot. I was trying to focus on the questions and not the monitor. They were asking about my last period, and I couldn't remember the date. We had to use a ballpark guess because my tablet had mysteriously lost the data from my calendar which I track monthly. I'm all for using technology for memory expansion, and we both failed to recall during the moment of need. *Figures!*

As I chattered away, the doctor listened, as she intently watched the screen. I was still talking when she announced,

"Congratulations! There is one *very* active baby in there! By the ultrasound, you're measuring ten weeks pregnant." It was like the words were delayed in the atmosphere and took a while to sink in. Then beating loudly and clearly, was the beautiful drumming of a rapid little heartbeat. I was stunned as they printed off the pictures of my very *alive*, and active little miracle. They estimated the baby was due August 20th. The nurse handed me the ultrasound images, and it was as if I was handed pure gold.

Conversation followed about my risks being high, due to age and miscarriage history. She wanted me to also see the high risk OBGYN for consult. I was impervious to the statistics and the recommended genetic testing. I had no desire to know about possible genetic defects but did love the idea of the ultrasounds that came with high risk pregnancies. I knew from my pregnancy with Haidyn, they give extra peeks along the way. The doctor recommended I at least have the Down Syndrome test, which was done via special ultrasound measurements. It was better for the baby to know prior to delivery, if he or she had it. It would help the doctors be better prepared during labor and delivery, if there were any medical concerns that needed to be addressed like heart issues, etc. Since it was only an ultrasound, I consented and declined everything else.

Mark and I left the office with the photo evidence in hand of our little secret. The symptoms all made sense now. There was *life* in my womb. Not a barely alive, but a *very* active life. I also don't believe the ten-week age of the baby was a coincidence either. It was at nine weeks when I went for the ultrasound for John Mark only to discover that he died around seven weeks. Unlike my other three pregnancies, I only had to wait two weeks to get past the first trimester. This seemed to be the biggest of all the remaining ominous hurdles placed along the pregnancy. Only time and faith could peel back the fear of *what if*.

## Chapter 8 - A Well-Timed Word

*A man finds joy in giving an apt reply and
how good is a timely word!
Proverbs 15:23 (NIV)*

About a week and half after the doctor's appointment, my family and I attended a conference at our church. It was a prophecy conference. I wasn't sure what to expect since I'd never been to one before. I was excited, but also a little nervous. The teaching was phenomenal! The guest speaker Ed Traut was a friend of the pastors. I found out he visits regularly and has been for years. The irony about meeting him at the conference in Kentucky is where he currently lives. His home is only three miles from where we lived in San Antonio. We had never heard of him until after moving to Kentucky.

At the end of Prophet Traut's teaching that evening, he began speaking to people in the audience. He shared different things about their past, present and future; very personal insights that only applied to them. It wasn't embarrassing, but something that would only have meaning to the person to whom he was speaking. It was amazing and edifying. I had learned awhile back that the biblical gift of prophecy isn't a freaky fortune telling ability, but a gift to be used to build and strengthen the church. I was seeing it in action. Intrigued by his insights, I watched and listened as the people validated what was said. His reputation is one for accuracy.

I sat on the front row amazed while silently praying he would pick me. At the same time, I also hoped that he wouldn't. It was only February 1st. I was afraid the secret would be outed. Mark and I, along with the doctor's office, were still the only people privy. We were impatiently waiting for Valentine's Day, so we could tell Haidyn of her special gift of a baby brother or sister. By then, I would be fourteen weeks pregnant and well into the second trimester.

As the evening wrapped up, Prophet Traut asked the pastor to pick someone from the audience. I was in direct line of sight across from where they were sitting, and immediately I heard my name called. It was excitement and dread at the same time. Haidyn was sitting right next to me, so she would hear everything that was said. Nervously I waited for his word for me. I never thought I needed to ask the Lord to be quiet.

The following is an excerpt from our prophetic word received that night. It would be used over the next months for comfort, strength and spiritual warfare. Every time fear would rear its ugly head, I would cling to these words and say them out loud. I know God's promise is more powerful than Satan's lies!

**Ed:** Michelle? Michelle in the front. Hi Michelle in the front. Are you married Michelle in the front? Are you married to Mr. in the front?
**Michelle:** I am, but I don't know where he is now.
**Ed:** Have you lost your husband?
**Michelle:** I think he might be in the bookstore. There he is. His name is Mark.
**Ed:** Mark. God is looking for you Mark.
**Michelle:** That's the question Mark...
**Ed:** Oh gosh. So, Michelle what do you do?
**Michelle:** I'm a marketing and advertising person.
**Ed:** You're a marketing and advertising person. How many children do you have?
**Michelle:** One.
**Ed:** Are you planning anymore?
**Michelle:** God willing.
**Ed:** The reason I'm saying that is there's been a decree in the heavenlies of God's, to you and your womb. God is visiting your body again. You'll have a baby. It's God's promise to you. In fact, it's a supernatural intervention of God. He's going to do something for you. Nothing is too hard for the LORD. Do you understand?
**Michelle:** I do.
**Ed:** God's going to do it for you. That's the will of the Lord. A decree in the heavens. So, it will be so. Michelle you're a remarkable lady. You're remarkable and God thanks you. He thanks you for all that you have done and put up with your whole life. The people that were against you, you always had the right attitude and the right spirit. He's going to reward you. You're a great mom. This baby is going to be reward from heaven that you know this year He is going to touch your womb in the most phenomenal way...Thank You, Jesus!

## Chapter 9 - The Big Reveal

*For nothing is secret that will not be revealed, nor anything hidden that will not be known and come to light.*
*Luke 8:17 (NKJV)*

Valentine's Day!! The day for the big reveal finally arrived. It was a good thing because I was starting to show. Hiding the pregnancy was becoming difficult. Apparently, this baby didn't want to remain a secret.

With gift bags and flowers in place on the breakfast table, we got Haidyn up for school earlier than usual. I intentionally layered gifts inside the bag so her "I'm Going to Be a Big Sister" shirt was on the bottom. I've never had more angst over buying a shirt. With the reassurance of the ultrasound and prophetic word, I refused to give into the fear and bought the shirt again.

We filmed Haidyn while she casually took out each gift. I wanted her to hurry up and get to the bottom of the bag, but also wanted to savor the moment. This would be the theme of this pregnancy. I waited a long time for this. Not so patiently, I watched as she looked at each item. When she finally pulled out the shirt, she gave us a quizzical look. She didn't act very surprised and she thought we were preparing for the baby mentioned by Prophet Traut. We explained that she didn't have to wait nine months. She was going to be a sister around August 20th. That provoked a reaction!

Tweenager that she was, the first thing she asked was if she could tell her friends. We laughed and told her that she could spread the news *after* we informed the family. Following early morning calls to family and close friends, I posted the announcement on Facebook. Needless to say, everyone was surprised! Forty-four years old and pregnant...It was my most-liked and commented-on post of the year.

## Chapter 10 - Look Momma!

*For You formed my inward parts; You covered me in my mother's womb. I will praise You, for I am fearfully and wonderfully made; marvelous are Your works, and that my soul knows very well. My frame was not hidden from You, when I was made in secret, and skillfully wrought in the lowest parts of the earth. Your eyes saw my substance, being yet unformed. And in Your book they all were written, the days fashioned for me, when as yet there were none of them. How precious also are Your thoughts to me, O God! How great is the sum of them! Psalms 139:13-17 (NKJV)*

Shortly after going public, the next few months seemed like a blur of revolving doctors' appointments, labs and ultrasounds. I was co-doctored by my primary OB and the high-risk physician. This doubled the prenatal visits. They tested me immediately for gestational diabetes. I flunked again. So, on came the dietician, restricted diet, and self-inflicted, multiple-finger stab wounds from glucose testing. I was also diagnosed with a severe Vitamin D deficiency after complaining about extreme exhaustion and joint pain.

I thought my iron was off, but this sun loving, normally very tan turned white girl, was lacking rays after moving from Texas to Kentucky. I was *severely* deficient, which brought on its own bailiwick of miserable symptoms.

After the first ultrasound blew my menopausal theory, and spotlighted our miracle, the time came for the next peek. It was an optional ultrasound, courtesy of the high-risk doctor. It was a special scan for Down Syndrome. The scan uses screening measures to check for specific markers on the baby which may indicate chromosomal issues.

Honestly, I opted to have the ultrasound more for reassurance of life, than concerns about genetic deficiencies. Even though the devil liked to taunt me with those fears because I was an older pregnant mom, I just wanted to see the baby again, and make sure he or she was still alive.

The day before the appointment, I received a call from the receptionist at the high-risk doctor's office. There was a change in his surgical calendar and they needed to reschedule the ultrasound. It was postponed until the following week. I was disappointed. I kept telling myself, *it is only a week.* It was too soon to feel the baby move, and I was counting on the ultrasound for reassurance of what I couldn't feel. Sounds a lot like faith, huh? And a downside of faith is not having anything tangible to go on. It must be exercised and escorted by trust. Unfortunately, my trust was still limping from the emotional wounds. Note doubt isn't the opposite of faith. It is certainty. I had to decide if I was going to live in fear for the next few months, or rest in

God's promise that I would have a child this year. I had to trust Him again.

When the time came for the ultrasound, the technician at check-in seemed perplexed when I gave her my due date. Apparently, this scan is so sensitive; it can only be done during a very small window of time during the pregnancy. Thanks to the doctor's reschedule, I was a week outside of the limit to conduct the test.

It was almost as if the Lord was ushering me past everyone's spoken concerns and fears regarding the baby's potential defects and issues with my age. Even well-meaning coworkers mentioned how sweet Down Syndrome babies are, as if to prepare me. Take note, no matter the woman's age this is something that no pregnant mother wants to hear...*Ever!*

Undeterred by the missed window of time, the tech brought me, Mark and Haidyn back for the ultrasound. They wanted to check on the baby. I soon realized that it wasn't just a routine check. As I listened to her, it became clear that we weren't out of the woods yet from their perspective regarding chromosomal concerns. She mentioned potential heart issues, webbing of the hands or feet, which could be seen in the ultrasound, if a chromosomal disorder was present...I half listened, as I climbed onto the table and waited. From my perspective, they were worrying about something arbitrary. I was in suspended animation waiting for any movement to show on screen and sounds of a precious beating heart.

Within seconds of the equipment touching my abdomen, you could hear a steady heartbeat. The tech even made comments about the baby showing off when she checked the heart's chambers. It was a healthy, strong heart with nothing missing or broken. It was perfect according to the tech. Satisfied with the health of the heart, she moved on to check the other body parts of the baby. Who by the way was very much alive and well, and didn't care to be bothered while attempting to sleep.

Even though a little early, they suspected the gender. Time would tell on the accuracy of the gender reveal, but one of the most precious images was taken right before ending the session. The tech managed to capture a perfect image of a little hand. She even mentioned that it was the best hand shot she had ever seen. It was as if the baby was saying, *Look Momma, five fingers! No worries...*No webbing, no deformities, a perfect and precious little hand that was fearfully and wonderfully made, and it was His blessed assurance that all is well.

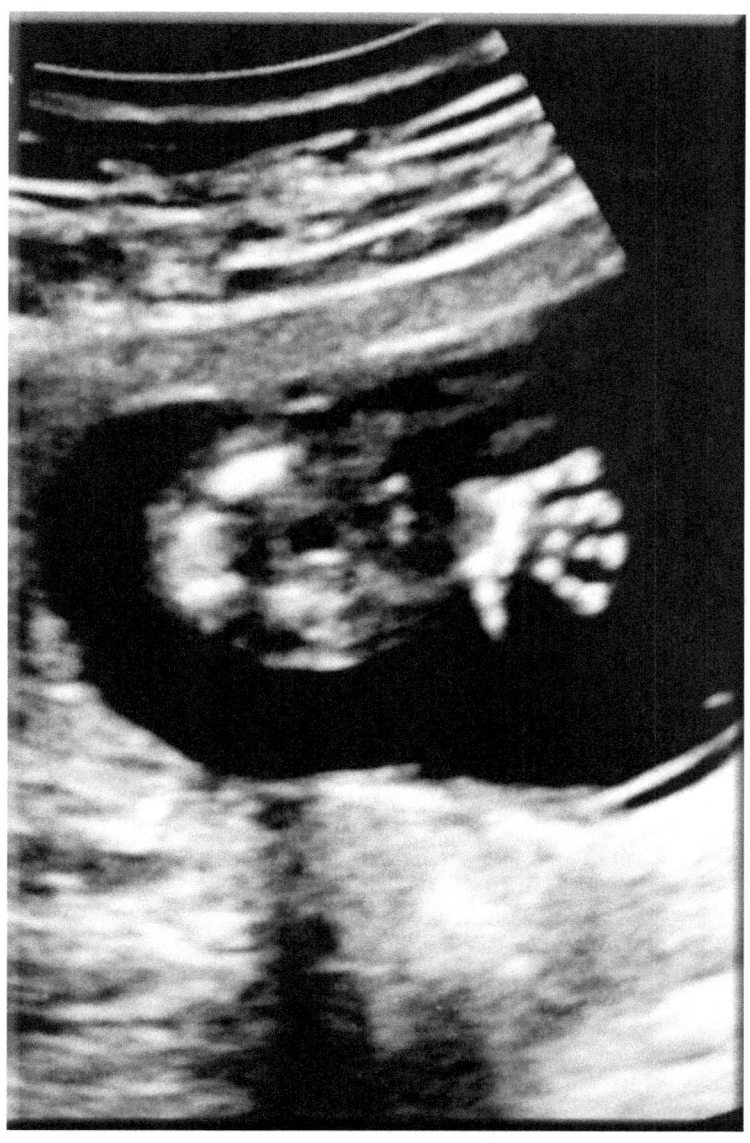

FIGURE 5: CARIS SOPHIA CHUDY
14 WEEK ULTRASOUND

## Chapter 11 - It's a Girl!

*Listen, O daughter, consider and give ear: Forget your people and your father's house. The king is enthralled by your beauty; honor him, for he is your lord. The Daughter of Tyre will come with a gift, men of wealth will seek your favor. All glorious is the princess within [her chamber]; her gown is interwoven with gold. In embroidered garments she is led to the king; her virgin companions follow her and are brought to you. They are led in with joy and gladness; they enter the palace of the king. Your sons will take the place of your fathers; you will make them princes throughout the land. I will perpetuate your memory through all generations; therefore, the nations will praise you for ever and ever.*
*Psalms 45:10-17 (NIV)*

After practically missing the first trimester, the pregnancy seemed to scream by as time to prepare crumbled. It was so surreal that I was pregnant and making changes to accommodate a baby. Changes also included new room assignments at the house.

Much to Haidyn's dismay, she was losing her playroom that featured her beloved dry-erase board, which is painted on the wall. For whatever reason, she was enamored with it. It would soon become the nursery. As a vanishing only child, she was having a hard time grappling the notion that most kids don't get two rooms for themselves.

Note I'm second of four, so I didn't have much empathy for her situation. However, my sibling culture taught me the value of negotiation. Haidyn would get a "hang spot" in the basement (after definition provided by one-said preteen) in exchange for her playroom for her and her friends to "ya know, hang". Of course, this spot, *must* include a new dry-erase board.

Exactly one month later, our growing family packed into the ultrasound room for the gender reveal. Names were vetted and approved by the majority (Mom and Dad), with a dissenting vote on the boy's name. My heart wasn't set on a preference, but I definitely wanted to know. I'm a planner and couldn't handle the post-birth gender surprise. I was already behind the planning curve by a trimester.

The baby was quickly becoming a family love affair. Mark, Haidyn and I loved seeing God's gift displayed on that little screen. Within minutes, we had more precious images with the tech's assurance that *it's a girl!*

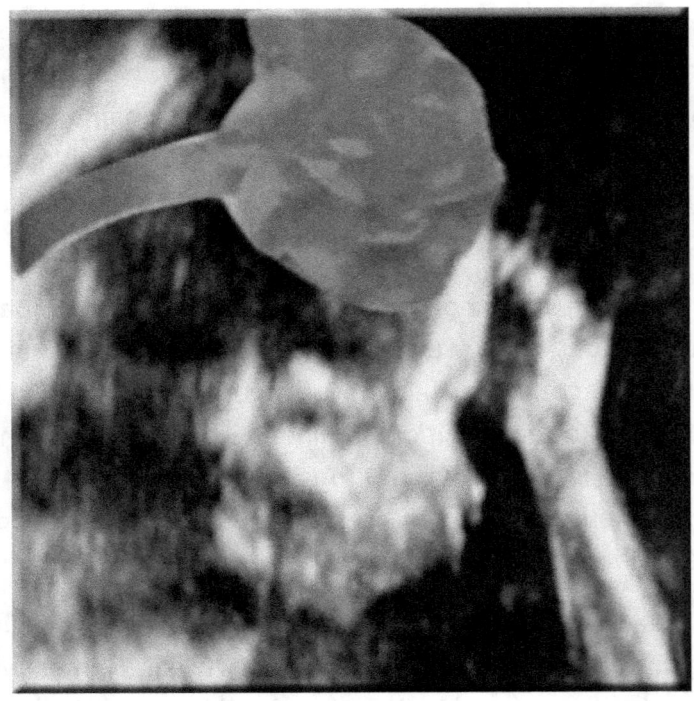

FIGURE 6: SHE'S A GIRL!
THE BIG REVEAL - MARCH 26, 2013

## Chapter 12 - Whispers from Heaven

*For as the heavens are higher than the earth, So are My ways higher than your ways, And My thoughts than your thoughts. Isaiah 55:9 (NKJV)*

Knowing that this pregnancy was a miracle, and God's special decree, He seemed to make special effort to deliver surprises along the way. They were like little kisses and love notes from heaven. Sent to encourage me and let me know He was involved in every detail, I was watchful and took notice when they came. They were often sent to counteract a worry or fear spoken over me about the baby. Like Jesus' mother Mary, I pondered them in my heart. Some people scoff at the supernatural, but I've witnessed too many things not to believe or at least let it pique my wonder. It would take more faith to deny His handiwork and presence.

During the pregnancy, I spent a lot of time on social media with my feet propped up. The swelling was horrendous and quite painful. Unfortunately, it started early in the pregnancy triggered by a plane trip to my niece's wedding. From six months on, it seemed to be a daily occurrence and required immediate intervention from my recliner, a stack of pillows, and my iPad. I would stay like that until my ankles morphed back into human form.

During my extended internet surfing, I noticed there were a lot of ultrasound images on my Facebook feed. Maybe I had a heightened sense of awareness because of my current state or maybe God was just extra busy dispatching blessings, but they were everywhere that spring and summer. A few in particular kept catching my eye. People were posting about faces seen in ultrasound photos, along with the baby's.

At first, I was doubtful and maybe a little cynical. I know the mind can play tricks on you and it can visualize form within the abstract. Just ask Rorschach about his ink blots. But then someone I know and respect, who was a month after me in their pregnancy, posted a picture of their ultrasound. It was as clear as the baby's face. It was another face that looked like a Roman bust alongside of their baby's face. Comments flew speculating the source. *Guardian angel? Technology fluke?* Nobody knew for sure, but there was no denying there was another face. And, then it was my turn.

It was the fourth ultrasound taken during the sixth month of pregnancy. As always, I was thrilled to have confirmation that my miracle was alive and well. She was peacefully resting with her hand in front of her mouth. This seemed to be a preferred position and still is today. Her little nose was easily made out. And then I noticed something peculiar. There was a profile of a face to the right of the baby. And not just any face…

*I couldn't believe it!* But it was hard to deny, since the face was familiar, especially the profile. It was distinct, and I saw it in the ultrasound photo. I kept staring at it. The profile looked like Anna's, my deceased mother-in-law, who passed in 1997.

I can't explain it nor am I advocating that Mark's deceased mother visited her granddaughter in the womb. But if you look at the ultrasound image, it looks like Grandma Anna is holding her grandbaby and whispering or singing to her while she slept.

Reality or not, it is a tender and very special photo. Anna passed away before we had children. There is something comforting knowing that heaven reaches down into our lives before we even leave the womb. The wonder of our heavenly life before and after this world was embodied in this picture. Knowing that His ways are higher and so are His thoughts, who am I to negate the possibility?

FIGURE 7: COULD IT BE...GRANDMA ANNA?
ABOVE: MARK CHUDY WITH HIS MOTHER ANNA CHUDY
BELOW: ULTRASOUND OF CARIS (LEFT) AND ANNA'S PROFILE (RIGHT)

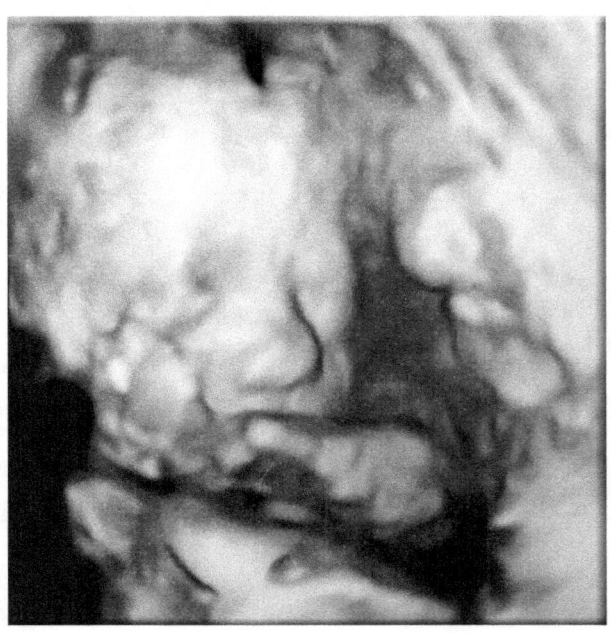

## Chapter 13 - Coaxed by Love

*For I am persuaded that neither death nor life, nor angels nor principalities nor powers, nor things present nor things to come, nor height nor depth, nor any other created thing, shall be able to separate us from the love of God which is in Christ Jesus our Lord.*
*Romans 8:38-39 (NKJV)*

As I continued to recover from life's battle wounds, my timid heart slowly started to trust. It was coming to life with each victory wrestled away from fear. God's love gently coaxed me to believe that all would be well. Each week further into the pregnancy or significant milestone cleared, I gained assurance that I was not being tricked...not tricked to feel, or lured into unrequited love, nor deceived through false hope.

I finally started to get excited and accepted my gift. I didn't care if I was twenty years older than most pregnant women. Joy started to flood into the deflated and dry areas of my heart with each decision to embrace His word delivered to me by Prophet Traut. This baby was my reward and God's promise to me, and He *always* keeps His promises!

So, with each ultrasound I got a glimpse of His gift. She was slowly being revealed. Even hints of her personality, along with likes and dislikes were captured.

When sleeping, she did NOT want to be bothered. Pictures were annoying. There were times we tried, we even paid to video her in 3D, and she would throw a leg over her face, so we couldn't get a good image. Try as we might to nudge, poke and shake her into position, she simply wouldn't comply. She's strong-willed and has a sense of humor with a little bit of sass. She's a hand girl. They were always near her face. We also discovered she's a thumb sucker, who prefers it to this day. She loves it to the point her thumb is cracking, and her cute little baby teeth are bucking. According to her, it tastes like cake. She gets rowdy before bedtime. She's high energy, very active and quite possibly a fancy dancer. I suspect she prefers tap.

With all of the insights gathered through ultrasound, her little self was taking shape in my heart and in our family. And then we chose the name. I couldn't believe how easy it was. With Haidyn I had multiple baby name books, spreadsheets, and polled friends and family input. For this one, it was swift and easily decided around the breakfast table in a day.

Before we found out the gender, Mark and I joked with Haidyn that if it's a boy his name would be Brock Lee Chudy. With a look of fear and exasperation she asked, "You're going to call him Broccoli? No! You can't call him that!" Spoken like a true teen who thinks her parents have lost their mind.

After much laughter at Haidyn's expense, Mark and I decided that we liked the name Brock. It was a strong masculine name, so we decided to keep it for the boy's choice. His full name would be Brock Nathaniel. Haidyn still wasn't a fan. For the girl's name, it was predetermined. We chose it years before when Haidyn was a toddler. Carson Sophia was chosen for our next baby girl. Haidyn must have gotten tired of waiting for an actual sister because she named her first doll Carson. Nine years after naming her doll we were going to repurpose it for the real deal. With multiple ultrasound confirmations of female gender, Carson Sophia was the winner for a girl.

Shortly after our naming session, I was at the office talking to one of my coworkers who was celebrating another grandbaby. Proudly displaying her picture, he mentioned her name was Charis. I remarked how beautiful and unique it was. I had never heard of the name. Somehow, I missed that Michael Douglas and Catherine Zeta Jones name their daughter the same years before, but with a variant spelling. My coworker said that his daughter chose it because of its meaning. Charis means grace, beloved and kindness. The significance of the meaning struck a heart chord in me.

Knowing how particular the LORD is with names, to the point of Him renaming people in the Bible, I decided to look up the meaning of Carson. A name has destiny implications. Sophia was chosen as a namesake for Mark's paternal grandmother. I knew Sophia meant wisdom but didn't have a clue about the meaning of Carson. I just liked how it sounded. So, after a quick name search I found the repugnant result of its meaning...swamp dweller.

*Oh, heck no!* I wasn't about to give my baby a name that means swamp dweller! I went back to my coworker and asked if he would mind me using his granddaughter's name in lieu of Carson. After I explained why, he laughed and consented. It didn't take anything to convince Mark and Haidyn to change. After creating our own spelling variation so it worked better with our last name, Caris Sophia was claimed. My beautiful gift and reward from God the Father was given a proclamation of destiny through her name as Grace, Beloved, Kindness and Wisdom.

I believe her name is what anchored my trust to His promise. It gave her an identity. All I needed after that was a little face to complete the image of who I held in my heart and felt in my womb. We were all waiting for Caris Sophia Chudy to take her rightful place in our home.

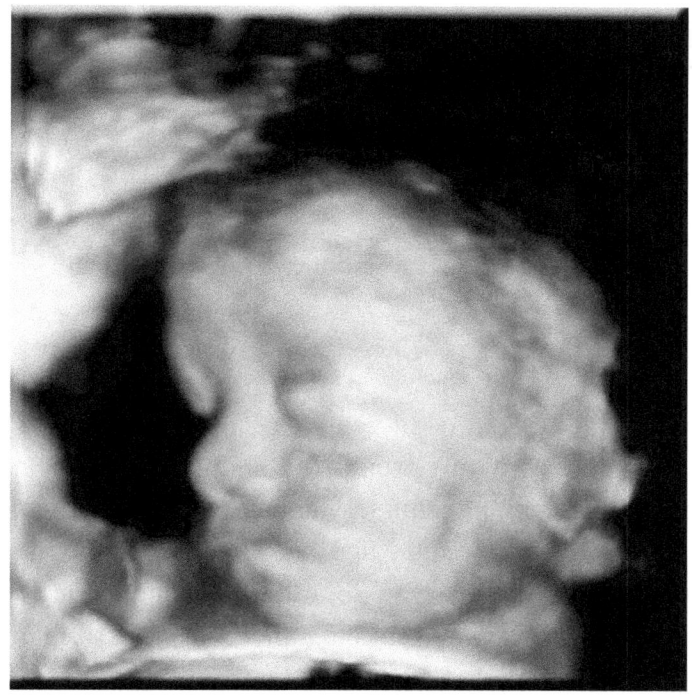

FIGURE 8: SLEEPING BEAUTY
CARIS SOPHIA - 27 WEEKS

## Chapter 14 - No Shopping Shame!

*Lift up your heads, you gates; be lifted up, you ancient doors, that the King of glory may come in. Psalm 24:7 (NIV)*

Running with my promise, I shopped! I took much pleasure in planning a nursery and completing my registry. That is, of course, once I figured out what all of the new gadgets were supposed to do. A lot had changed in twelve years! Haidyn was my shopping and baby registry partner, much to Mark's relief, because he hates to shop!

It was important to me for Haidyn to be part of the celebration and preparation. She is her mother's child and loves to plan! We brought her to most of the ultrasounds to ensure she didn't miss a thing. However, she's not only a planner; she also has a very tender heart.

When Haidyn learned about the miscarriages a few years after they happened, she was heartbroken. It was hard for me to watch her grieve years after I had emotionally shut down. But her sadness over the loss of her siblings was hard to hide. It made me wonder if I did the right thing by trying to shelter her from the pain. I wanted to wait until she was older to tell her...old enough to understand and better able to bear the grief.

But she is so smart; she figured it out on her own. Haidyn asked me point blank if I had ever lost a baby. I couldn't lie to her. So, I not only told her yes, but that she has two siblings in heaven. The pending arrival of her little sister brought healing not just for her, but for each of our aching hearts. The baby wasn't just for me, she was *our* baby.

So, there we were, going aisle to aisle, gleefully shopping in a place that I couldn't even make eye contact with a few months before. A place that once mocked me, and brought me much shame and emptiness, now welcomed me. Retail therapy is not just a term to be taken lightly or in jest. For some like myself, it was more than therapy or frivolous spending. It was my declaration of belief, and a public statement of reaffirmed trust in God.

The ultimate statement of my blessed assurance in His promise was the purchase of the bedding. It was still a sensitive subject. If you recall, I purchased the helicopter set for John Mark before we found out he was gone. Returning an item shouldn't be so painful, but just like any other store they asked the reason why for the return. And I answered the routine question with my unwanted reality and facts, "The baby died." Followed by, "I'm no longer pregnant. I have no need of the bedding." Underneath the hardness of my responses was grief wrapped in humiliation. The return was just another way of rubbing my nose in it.

I knew when I purchased this baby's bedding it would be a step of faith. And going public with my choices by posting on social media was my yes to His amen! There is something sweet and victorious about a public testimony of His faithfulness.

FIGURE 9: THE CRADLE AWAITS

## Chapter 15 - Showered with Sissy Love

*I will bless my people and their homes around my holy hill. And in the proper season I will send the showers they need. There will be showers of blessing.*
*Ezekiel 34:26 (NLT)*

Showers of blessing indeed! Don't ever discount the desires of a child who has a heart full of love that is only sourced by Jesus. Much to my delight, my budding, beautiful daughter Haidyn Elise and her twelve-year-old friends wanted to host my baby shower. Those girls never cease to amaze me with ingenuity and gusto. The world has no idea of the girl power that is about to be unleashed upon it!

At her insistence that she could do it, Haidyn gathered her closest friends and got to work. To give you part of my back story, event planning is in my professional marketing repertoire. The girl must have inherited some of those skills. She did a fabulous job! She made her momma proud. From handmade invitations, to a well-rounded guest list, a sniff-and-taste candy bar diaper quiz, timed bottle guzzling, the dreaded taste and name the baby food game, and even a homemade delicious strawberry cake, fun was had by all! Haidyn even surprised me with friends who drove hours to attend. It was a precious day and memory.

I must admit, it was very odd for me before the party started. Banned to my bedroom to wait for the festivities to begin, I sat rocking with my swollen feet propped up. I could hear them as they brought things in to decorate and set up. I'm not used to being on the receiving end of the party. It was kind of nice not to have to be the one in planning and execution mode. It definitely gave me time to ponder and appreciate the event, especially this one.

At forty-five, I didn't think I would ever again be the baby shower's honored guest. Parties thrown for people my age normally had over-the-hill balloons floating around. It was surreal that my sweet baby girl, now a young lady, was throwing me a baby shower...a pre-birthday party for her little sister. Life and God is good, and worthy of celebration. Thank you, my sweet, big brown-eyed, beautiful inside and out, Haidyn Elise...my true love girl (insert hug and kiss here)!

FIGURE 10: LITTLE MISS HOSTESS HAIDYN (AGE 12)

FIGURE 11: SHOWER BLESSING BY CLAUDIA CALVERT

## Chapter 16 - A Time to Wait

*For no matter how many promises God has made, they are "Yes" in Christ. And so through Him the "Amen" is spoken by us to the glory of God.*
*2 Corinthians 1:20 (NIV)*

With the due date quickly approaching, it also seemed like it would never arrive. Isn't it strange how the shortest amount of time can feel like an eternity when you're full of expectation? It didn't help that they kept changing my due date during the pregnancy. I was given three, but I was going with the first one because I believed it was the most accurate. However, there was a four-day window between estimates.

But there came a point when everything was in place, and I found myself waiting for my new-found love to arrive. The nursery was finally finished. Her name, Caris Sophia, was on the wall above the crib which was returned and replace three times. The special-order rocking chair was delivered and in place. The room was beautiful, but still empty and lifeless.

I sat rocking in the empty nursery looking around and realized the room felt flat. This room was the least used room in the house up until that point. There were no life marks imprinted on it. It's the people and the memories that make a home come to life. I was curious about the little person who was soon to arrive. She had a room waiting for her with her name on it, but only she could make it truly hers. I couldn't wait to meet her.

FIGURE 12: THE NURSERY

## Chapter 17 – Caris Eve... The Last Night of Chudy-Three

*For the revelation awaits an appointed time; it speaks of the end and will not prove false. Though it linger, wait for it; it will certainly come and will not delay.*
Habakkuk 2:3 (NIV)

The first one came and went, and then the second. As the third due date approached, the doctor started to get concerned. There were minimal signs of progress, and neither one of us was getting any smaller. This baby seemed quite content to stay where she was, even though there was little space left for her to conquer and inhabit. Mark and the doctor started to negotiate eviction. I was on the fence about messing with God's timeline, but willing to listen to arguments.

I also was not thrilled with having a Pitocin drip again. Twelve years later, I still remembered the intensity of the "Pit" contractions while laboring for Haidyn, which the Army doctor let me enjoy up until eight centimeters dilated, before he permitted the epidural. *And*, they also forgot to mention the bonus of post-pregnancy Pitocin swelling!

FYI ignorance is not always bliss. The only thing I knew back then came from the advice of my new neighbor Amy, whom I met when I was nine months pregnant. We had just moved into our new house. I received my first lesson on labor and delivery negotiation tactics while chatting in her driveway. She said to scream for an epidural, if the word Pitocin was mentioned. I wasn't even sure what Pitocin was, or if I was even going to have an epidural, but her words were amplified in my head by the hyper-intense contractions introduced by the doctor's Pitocin affinity and desire to finish his shift early. Contractions seemed to come like tsunami waves pounding me one after the other without pause, never giving time to breathe.

Now fast forward to the impending arrival of Caris, who seemed to need a little help from my Pitocin friend for her to enter the world. The doctor thought it was in our best interest to induce. It would also guarantee she would be the one to deliver. She was on call that weekend. I reluctantly agreed, as my aching joints cheered, and waited for the call to confirm the induction. They had a full house at the woman's hospital and it came down to availability. Mark and I left the office to wait.

Not even an hour after leaving, the nurse called with a room. We had to be there by 9 p.m. The timing was perfect. It was a Friday night. Haidyn had a football game to cheer, and we had plenty of time to attend, grab dinner and then head to the hospital. My sister Missy and brother-in-law Jerry had flown in from Texas and were also waiting for Caris Sophia's grand entrance. It was like déjà vu since they were also present for Haidyn's birth.

So, off we went to enjoy Haidyn's game on an unusually cool, August evening, otherwise known as Caris Eve. Life as we knew it for the past twelve years was about to transition into our next chapter. We would no longer be the family of Chudy-three, but Chudy-four. Haidyn would no longer be an only child. Mark and I would have to mind-shift to say "the girls" when referring to our children (plural). We had to make room for our blessing, in every area of our life, to include our thoughts and frame of reference.

As we all know, expansion can be uncomfortable even if it's good. And God's gifts don't always guarantee less pain and misery. Just ask Mary who traveled a great distance on the back of a donkey when great with child. And she wasn't carrying just any child; she was great with *His* Child, who happened to be God's only Son.

My pregnancy, as well, was not without discomfort or pain even though it was His reward. Thank God there were no required donkey rides! However, I was plagued with severe Vitamin D deficiency and extreme fatigue, as well as, daily obligatory multiple finger-sticks for glucose testing due to my second round of gestational diabetes. Sometimes the suffering makes you better appreciate the gift. Abundance can be minimized unless you're familiar with lack. The promise makes it worth pushing through the pain. When you know that the blessing is just on the other side, you truly grasp the significance of what you're waiting to receive.

For me, other than being forty-five and great with child, and my previously mentioned discomforts, I felt pretty good that night. I could only give the Lord credit for that. It could have been a very miserable pregnancy, if God hadn't intervened right after I conceived. We often don't realize the extent of His handiwork to get us ready for His plan until we glance back. The clarity is much better in hindsight.

Here's a little backstory (no pun intended) to help you better understand. For the last eight years, prior to getting pregnant, I dealt with excruciating back pain and all the ills that come with a ruptured lower lumbar disc...constant pain, poor sleep, lifting and life restrictions, limited range of motion, and so on. Fear of the pain and fear of re-injury was a whole other topic. I knew if I ever got pregnant, there was potential for much discomfort and severe pain on top of the pregnancy norms. But thank God, He completely healed my back only weeks after I conceived, and before I even realized I was pregnant!

Looking back, it's amazing to see how God prepared me to carry the blessing. My pastor went to Israel in January 2013. He sent videos back over social media, so we could experience the trip along with him. He also sent word that the anointing was so strong when he visited the Western Wall, he wanted to bring our prayer requests there to pray over them. He asked for people to post their prayer requests on his timeline before he returned to the Wall. I jumped on it!

I had gone for prayer for healing of my back so many times that I'd lost count. But I was determined, and believed that Jesus would eventually heal me, so I kept asking. And by the grace of God, it manifested right after I conceived. What I thought was a reward for my faith, was also His way of preparing me to be His chosen vessel to carry His greatest treasure...His beloved charis (a.k.a. Caris) treasure, an act of favor, full of grace, kindness and wisdom, and His earthly tabernacle. It was almost time for her arrival.

Mark, Jerry, Missy, Haidyn and I made it a point not to linger when the game ended so we could get dinner before heading to the hospital. I knew it may be my last decent meal for the next couple of days. Everything was smooth sailing until we assumed that there would be restaurants still open. By God's grace, a very nice manager stayed open to feed us once he found out where we were headed. They were already closed, but he forgot to lock the door.

So, with full stomachs, we made our way over to the hospital for what I have to admit was the worst night's sleep I've ever had in my life. And if you knew how poorly I usually sleep, that says a lot! I don't even think what I had would qualify as sleep.

When they finally got me into a room after checking in, they strapped me up to so many monitors I felt like a tethered whale. With every flip and flop, some tracking device would detach, and the nurse would come in to hook it back up. That action normally required waking me up to replace the gadget or cord. Since Caris wasn't making any effort to come out, they had to attempt to soften my cervix. I flipped and flopped all night on a bed that felt like a mattress stuffed with concrete. I found out later that I was "sleeping" on a labor and delivery bed which was not supposed to be restful. It was a place of labor, not rest; a place of labor indeed. For me, it was a labor motivated by love and fueled by His promise. I wanted my reward, and it was worth losing a night's sleep.

FIGURE 13: CARIS EVE
AUGUST 23, 2013

## A Time to Sing

*by Michelle Renée Chudy*

"Sing, barren woman, you who have never bore a child; burst into song, shout for joy, you who were never in labor; because more are the children of the desolate woman than of her who has a husband," says the LORD.
Isaiah 54:1 (NIV)

## Chapter 18 - Labor of Love

*We remember before our God and Father your work produced by faith, your labor prompted by love, and your endurance inspired by hope in our Lord Jesus Christ.*
*1 Thessalonians 1:3 (NIV)*

Early Saturday morning, my doctor arrived to check me and to validate progress. There wasn't any. Much to everyone's disappointment, especially for sleep-deprived me, the cervix softening meds were not working. Plan B was implemented and followed by the dreaded Pitocin.

Now, without going into gory details, it is very true that all pregnancies are different. That includes labor and delivery. I felt this one in places that no pain should ever be felt. Blame it on age, years of wear and tear, or whatever reason you can think of, I felt *every* contraction to its fullest, and in places where I've never previously had pain in my life. The curse is real folks! God was NOT joking when He told Eve He would intensify labor pains, and she would bear children in anguish. Pitocin is an agent of the curse and paves the way to anguish!

You can ask most who know me; I have a pretty high tolerance for pain and avoid meds, if possible. And, I've had my share of sports and life injuries, to include a partially torn Achilles tendon, and a ruptured lumber disc and fractured neck, which pale in comparison. I now know what hard labor and intense pain feels like. Haidyn's labor was a cake walk compared to Caris'. And guess where the contractions manifested after the doctor broke my water? My lower back, of course! Remember my earlier comment about fear of the back pain? Well, back-pain spasm flashbacks, coupled with Pitroid contractions, are a whole 'nother level of pain! It made me forget about my healing and almost made me forget my Christianity. It also made me a little mean and a lot angry. Note I'm not a crier when hurt. I like to retaliate and attack the source of pain. Since that wasn't an option, I was more than ready for the epidural. But like the dangling carrot to tease the horse, it kept moving out of reach.

Prior to labor the hospital staff assured me, *You can have it upon asking. We won't make you wait*, they said. So, around five centimeters I asked, and, they said...NO! Apparently, there is some unwritten rule that you must have two bags of IV fluid before you could have an epidural. That was never mentioned. We were at only one bag. I was not amused. So, at seven centimeters, and before I cussed at anyone and lost my Christian ways, they finally obliged. It's funny (not really), what pain can reveal in a person. It also makes you reconsider what you're willing to do to relieve yourself from it. I was definitely relieved and a lot nicer when the epidural worked.

Unfortunately, even though the intensity of the contractions was masked by the epidural, they were just as strong as ever. And with each intense contraction, Caris' heart rate dropped and wasn't recovering as quickly as it should. The doctor became concerned. My friendly and normally conversational OBGYN became very businesslike. She watched the monitor while checking me. The baby started to show signs of distress.

Unbeknownst to me, the baby was lodged behind my pubic bone. The doctor wanted to honor my wishes about letting me do the work, but she was getting prepared to intervene. An emergency C-section was now imminent if the baby remained lodged, or if I couldn't push Caris out in less than 30 minutes. And with the strength from Jesus, and help from a little suction, we met the deadline. Caris Sophia entered the world on August 24th at 4:24 p.m. in perfect health!

After suctioning her, they immediately put her on my chest to bond. It seemed surreal that she was finally here. I saw the sweet little face that belonged to a part of my heart that was already filled with love for her. My heart wasn't taken away from Haidyn or anyone else that held its stock. A dormant area expanded with love that was reserved only for Caris Sophia.

As I held my precious baby girl, I was in awe of the gift I was given. There were so many emotions, but also a quieting of something deep within me. At that moment emptiness was filled, yearning answered, and grief finally laid to rest. She wasn't a replacement, but a fulfillment. Peace and contentment visited room 265 that day. I delivered Caris Sophia, but through Caris Sophia, Jesus delivered me. He also brought healing to our family through a baby, which seems to be God's preferred way. You could see it on each of our faces as we held her. Caris Sophia was an ambassador. She stood in the gap for her brother and sister, who dwell in Paradise, and wait for us.

As I snuggled my baby girl, I soon realized why she was lodged during labor. The ultrasound lied. She was nowhere close to the size indicated the week before. She weighed a pound plus more than projected. She was solid! I like to tell people that God stuffed her full of good things before sending her my way. Of course, the almost daily blizzards and more than occasional cheeseburgers probably didn't help. Which by the way, this was the celebratory meal my husband brought me a couple of hours after giving birth!

FIGURE 14: SHE'S HERE! OUR FAMILY OF FOUR
AUGUST 24, 2013

# Chapter 19 - The Father's Hand

*And I give them eternal life, and they shall never perish; neither shall anyone snatch them out of My hand. My Father, who has given them to Me, is greater than all; and no one is able to snatch them out of My Father's hand. I and My Father are one. John 10:28-30 (NKJV)*

There are some things in life that only a picture can express what would take a multitude of words to say. When Caris Sophia was barely a day old, the hospital photographer captured one of the most precious and profound moments. It is the essence of my earthly journey, the destiny of my children, and the resting place to all He calls His own. This photo tells the heart of Father God and how He cares for us.

With complete tenderness and love, He holds us like a newborn babe in the palm of His hand. A strong, capable hand that holds love, life, hopes, sorrows and dreams. It is patient and willing, and waits for us to entrust our life to Him and be held. And for those of us who choose to trust in Jesus, no one can snatch us away. There is no safer place to be than resting in our Father's hand.

FIGURE 15: RESTING IN DADDY'S HAND
CARIS SOPHIA CHUDY - 1 DAY YOUNG

# Chapter 20 – Introducing... Caris Sophia Chudy

---

*For this child I prayed; and the LORD has granted me my petition which I asked of Him. 1 Samuel 1:27 (NKJV)*

CARIS SOPHIA

(CARE-iss) [Meaning: grace, kindness, beloved]
(so-FEE-ya) [Meaning: wisdom]

Daughter of the King of Kings. Decreed in the heavenlies from God to the womb. His promise. A supernatural intervention. A reward from above.
A good and perfect gift who came down from the Father of Lights. A light to the world, brilliant, radiant, bright. His glory will be seen upon you.
Gentiles shall come to your light.

For this child I prayed; and the LORD has given me my petition which I asked of Him. – 1 Samuel 1:27

## Chapter 21 - The Stocking

*And we know that in all things God works for the good of those who love Him, who have been called according to His purpose. Romans 8:28 (NIV)*

I bought this stocking over twelve years ago when I bought Haidyn's. This was in anticipation of future child, number two. Each year, I would find it tucked in the Christmas tote, sigh to myself, and put it back in with the unused decorations.

Each year the sigh got smaller and hope a little flatter. I almost gave the stocking away Christmas 2012, not even aware my miracle baby was already growing inside of me. On December 5, 2013, as a testament of God's faithfulness, the stocking was hung with care with Caris' name stitched upon it. God is good and still works on behalf of those who love Him!

FIGURE 16: THE STOCKING OF HOPE

## Chapter 22 - Holy Visitations

*See that you do not look down on one of these little ones. For I tell you that their angels in heaven always see the face of my Father in heaven.*
*Matthew 18:10 (NIV)*

Two days after Caris turned thirteen months old, something *amazing* happened during the night. Mark and I were downstairs watching a movie. Around midnight Caris woke up crying. For the past couple of weeks, this was a regular event and she did this around the same time. Night crying supposedly was common for her stage of development. I went into her room to check on her as usual, but this time I found her on her knees facing the back of the crib and crying really hard. She seemed scared.

I picked her up and took her to the chair to rock and console her. She grabbed her "napkin" (a burp cloth) off the chair arm and held it while we rocked. After a few minutes, she calmed down. I put her back in the crib on her back, with "baby" (a stuffed giraffe that has an attached blanket embroidered with "Jesus Loves Me"), on her left side. Before walking out, I draped her blanket over her, kissed her, and then went back downstairs.

About thirty minutes later, over the monitor I heard her cry and whimper again, and then she became quiet. I assumed she finally fell asleep. When the movie was over, which was around 1:00 a.m., I made my usual rounds to the girls' rooms to kiss them each goodnight. When I went into Caris' room, the napkin immediately caught my attention. It was neatly draped over the front crib rail, perfectly positioned in the center. I found it odd because I normally fling it over the side rail. And, it's nowhere near straight when I do it.

When I looked at Caris, she was peacefully sleeping on her *tummy* with the blanket pulled all the way up and tucked firmly in around her sides down to her legs. It was a perfect tuck on both sides without a gap or crease. *I never tuck her in like that!* I just drape the blanket over her. What was even more amazing was her baby was tucked in too, just like she was!

I brought Mark in to show him and asked, "Did you do this?" He said, "No, I haven't been in the room." The first thing that came to mind was John 20:7, and how Jesus took the time to neatly fold His face napkin, or shroud, when He rose from the dead. I immediately sensed angelic activity. Every night I pray over Caris, and I plead the blood of Jesus. I ask Him to sing over her, and for His guardian angels to watch over her so she doesn't make a peep. Why would I not expect Him to answer that prayer?

The next morning when Haidyn woke up, I asked her if she went into Caris' room the night before, even though I knew she didn't. As I suspected, she hadn't gone in either. I know, that I know, my specially decreed baby received a holy visitation that night! Still amazed, I thanked Jesus all the next day for comforting her and tucking her in.

There were two other times over the course of that year where Caris received visible angelic attention. Again, it was a crying and soothing situation. I would go to check on her and discover her angel had tucked her in again and she was sound asleep. Just to silence the skeptics, I asked Mark and Haidyn if they were the ones. I even went as far as trying to duplicate the seamless tuck. I couldn't do it!

Oh, the love of Jesus for His children, especially the little ones. He cares so much about us it never ceases to amaze me! And I learn so much about Him, through the love and life of a small and wondrous child. May I never lose the wonder of my glorious Savior.

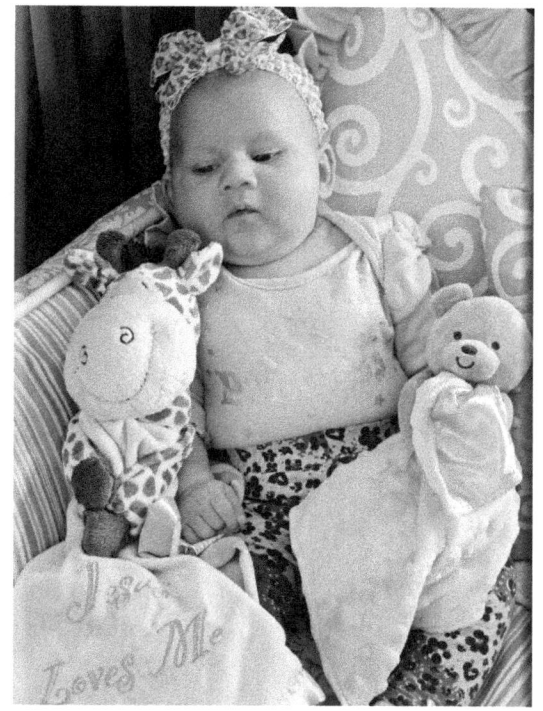

FIGURE 17: "BABY" AND PRINCESS CARIS SOPHIA
10 WEEKS YOUNG

## Chapter 23 - Great Expectations

*For we are God's masterpiece. He has created us anew in Christ Jesus, so we can do the good things He planned for us long ago. Ephesians 2:10 (NLT)*

*God has given each of you a gift from His great variety of spiritual gifts. Use them well to serve one another. Do you have the gift of speaking? Then speak as though God himself were speaking through you. Do you have the gift of helping others? Do it with all the strength and energy that God supplies. Then everything you do will bring glory to God through Jesus Christ. All glory and power to Him forever and ever! Amen.
1 Peter 4:10-11 (NLT)*

It's a curious thing to watch a child grow knowing that she arrived through a special decree from the One True God. I often catch myself studying her, wondering. With one eye on the temporal and the other on the eternal, I've learned to watch for glimpses of her gifting and destiny, as she blossoms into her God-given identity. I'm intrigued by her purpose and His plan for her life.

My sweet, easygoing baby, who slept through the night starting at eleven days old, is now a high-energy toddler. She's extremely intelligent, mostly polite, with a memory like an elephant, and has an impish sense of humor. A repeated "No thank you!! NO THANK YOU!" was her running response to her pediatrician Doctor Ducklehead (a.k.a. Dr. Hood) when she was about to receive her shots. Her most recent hilarious, proclamation while eating Chinese was, "I said I don't like it. PERIOD!" This was her adaptation from listening to us voice text and insert punctuation.

Caris delights us and keeps us on our toes. Unlike Haidyn, who would stay where you told her to stay, and asked permission to eat candy, Caris just does what she wants, when she wants and goes where she wants. An exasperated "Caris Sophia!" followed by a sigh, is often heard, just as much as outbursts of laughter over something she's said or done. But the wisdom in me makes me hide the scissors and markers and restrict the use of crayons unless closely supervised. So far, this strategy has protected hair and most of the walls from her artistic expression.

She's loving and lovable, very snuggly, and quite a bit stubborn with a strong sense of self. There is no doubt she is a leader, but it's balanced with a tender and kind heart. She notices the smallest of details and isn't shy about sharing her joy and wonder, as well as, immediate dislike. However, we often need to remind Caris that she is not in charge...yet. It was recently prophesied about how she would try to sway the home because she is a natural leader. This is one prophetic word I wish I could rewind and press pause until she turns eighteen. Ever since it was given, swaying not only exacerbated, it practically manifested full-force seemingly overnight! Often a battle of will ensues, and I have to remind myself that I'm not subject to a three-foot tall dictator wearing a Minnie Mouse nightgown. There are reports that I can be a little stubborn myself, but the child gives me a run for the money.

That same prophetic word, also said that we would see miracles happen through her at a very young age because of her crazy gift of faith. We are to teach her the simple way of miracles. So, when I'm shopping with this crazy faith-filled two-year-old, and she asks to pray over strangers in the store, I heed her request. I stop what I'm doing to ask the person if she can pray for them.

It first happened while visiting San Antonio, and it caught me off guard. My first reaction was to say, *no, don't bother anyone*, but I didn't. I can be bold, but my natural introverted tendencies are to keep to myself. However, in my spirit, I paused because I knew not to discount the purity of a child's action wanting to petition God on behalf of another. I also knew that Caris was His instrument and can impart His healing.

So awkwardly, I approached Caris' first assignment and said, "Excuse me ma'am, my baby would like to pray for you. Would that be okay?" The reaction is always one of surprise but followed by a hesitant yes. Caris then touches their hand or arm by her own volition, and prays, "Be healed in Jesus' name." Or she prays, "Bless you in Jesus' name." It's a simple prayer, whispered from the lips of a baby who has the faith of a giant.

I've noticed that her requests are not random, but specific. Caris says, "We need to pray for her Mommy." I ask which one, and she'll point to the person. It's never the one close by, but someone across the store she has set her eyes and faith upon. So, in the routine of our day, God shows up through the hands and prayers of a little child. It's amazing how God uses my children to draw me and my Christianity out into the world, and I know the best is yet to come.

FIGURE 18: STROLLER & SUN KISSES

## A Gift

Now that you know part of my story, I'd love to share more. Here is a gift for you. It's an excerpt from my autobiography ***The Battle of Surrender: One Woman's Journey to Sacrifice.***
Go to this link to download your free ebook preview:
http://bit.ly/SongBattleofSurrender

Blessings!

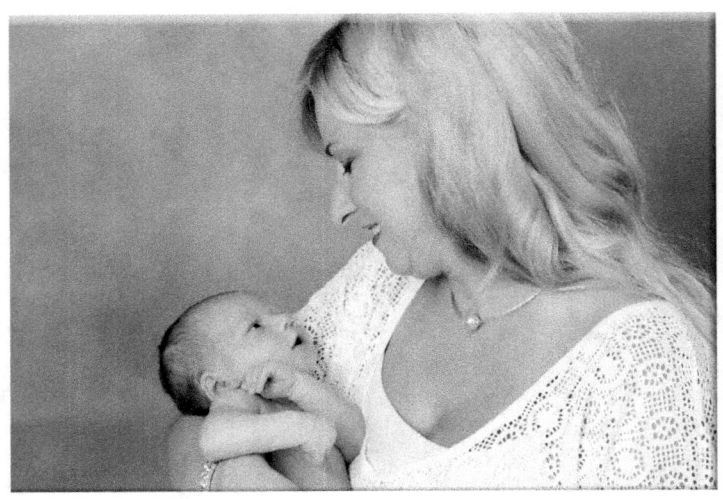

FIGURE 19: CARIS SOPHIA & MOMMOM MICHELLE
11 DAYS AND 45 YEARS YOUNG

FIGURE 20: HEAVEN SENT CARIS SOPHIA
11 DAYS YOUNG

FIGURE 21: CARIS SOPHIA CHUDY
4 MONTHS YOUNG

FIGURE 22: HAIDYN ELISE & CARIS SOPHIA
12 YEARS & 4 MONTHS YOUNG

FIGURE 23: TALKING TO JESUS
CARIS SOPHIA - 8 MONTHS YOUNG

FIGURE 24: DADDY PRINCE CHARMING MARK & PRINCESS CARIS SOPHIA
46 YEARS & 8 MONTHS YOUNG

FIGURE 25: BIRTHDAY GIRL!
1 YEAR YOUNG

FIGURE 26: LITTLE MISS SASS
CARIS SOPHIA - 2 YEARS YOUNG

FIGURE 27: BEAUTIFUL GIRL IN MY WORLD
CARIS SOPHIA - 2 YEARS YOUNG

FIGURE 28: SHE CAN DO AMAZING THINGS!
CARIS SOPHIA - 3 YEARS YOUNG

FIGURE 29: OUR SWEET GIRL
CARIS SOPHIA - 4 YEARS YOUNG

FIGURE 30: SISTER LOVE
HAIDYN ELISE 16 YEARS & CARIS SOPHIA 4 YEARS YOUNG

FIGURE 31: THE CHUDY BEAUTIES
CHRISTMAS 2017

FIGURE 32: OUR SWEET & SASSY GIFT
CARIS SOPHIA CHUDY

FIGURE 33: GOD MAKES ALL THINGS MERRY & BRIGHT! OUR GIFTS!!
HAIDYN & CARIS CHUDY

## A Time to Be Comforted

> *All praise to God, the Father of our Lord Jesus Christ. God is our merciful Father and the source of all comfort. He comforts us in all our troubles so that we can comfort others. When they are troubled, we will be able to give them the same comfort God has given us.*
> *1 Corinthians 1: 3-4 (NLT)*

As I continue to walk the path of recovery, I have found as I've shared my miscarriage story with others, there are *many* who have suffered the same loss. I've also discovered that each journey is unique. Where I was devastated by my first and deflated by the second, a close friend expressed that it was her third that set desperation in her soul.

What became clear through my research was grief, introduced by miscarriage, is often not expressed. Like a cultural taboo, people shy away from the subject. Closure is elusive due to lack of burial. The expectation is to move on with life as if the pregnancy and loss never happened. Though journeys are unique, many common threads tie us together in our experience. Some people were left in bondage to fear of future miscarriages, others wrestled with the tremendous weight of unexpressed sorrow. Anger, shame, embarrassment, guilt, detachment and frustration over unanswered questions plagued most of us, too. Condolences were notably lacking in most stories. I also found that comfort and healing were exchanged each time, when a personal miscarriage testimony was shared.

Sadly, what I suffered through in isolation was experienced by many, but never given a voice. I was not alone, and neither are you if miscarriage is part of your life's journey. So, with the comfort that I've received, I give to you the same. **You are not alone!**

As you read the following, these are heart stories from women and men, who have elected to share their personal experience with miscarriage, stillborn birth, infertility struggles and loss of a child. I am honored and humbled to be entrusted with each one. I pray that you receive the same comfort God has given us. I offer to you the voice of pregnancy loss and miscarriage, and its testimony.

## Katie's Story

The first sign of blood was like a kick to the gut. You're not supposed to bleed like this when you're pregnant. It was like being torn in two...the physical pain warring with the pain in my heart as to which was going to split me first. When the reality of what was happening to us, to our baby, sank in...life was altered. Forever.

Babies. I didn't realize how much I longed for them until I lost my own. Sure, I always wanted to be a momma, but when I lost our first child...I felt the loss everywhere. My body ricocheted between overwhelmed with the heartache and numbness. Intense pain. Then nothing. There was a piece missing in my heart. I felt like I was wading through quicksand. I'd experienced loss before, grandparents moving on to Heaven, pets...but all were due to old age, they'd lived long fulfilling lives...my baby didn't. But THIS was the first time I'd experienced loss too soon. Unplanned. Unknown. Without warning. I couldn't wrap my head around it. We were in ministry. Youth Pastors. We prayed. We tithed. We loved Jesus with everything within us. Then why did we lose our baby? What did we do wrong? Did we have sin in our life? My mind was whirring like a top. Constantly spinning with question after question, doubt, confusion, pain, shame, loss, anger...I laid in bed for days afterwards in this whirlwind of chaos. I didn't leave our bedroom when people brought food or comfort by. Mark was the face of our grief while I hid in our bed. I understood why Jackie O wore that long dark veil when she laid her husband to rest...grief, at least in the beginning, is too private to share with those who don't already hold your heart.

As we began processing our loss I found solace and strength in the only constant life has...Him. I submerged myself in His word and His presence. A year later we became pregnant again. The *joy of that moment...exhilarating. Beautiful. Terrifying. We passed the nine-week mark of when we lost the first baby. We both let out a sigh of relief. It was time for our ultrasound...excitement, and some fear. But everything was going to be okay. He had us. Loved us. Blessed us. Then the bottom dropped out of our world. Again. No heartbeat. What? How? Why? I went straight to our church and threw myself on the Altar and cried out with everything in me. We needed a miracle. We needed our baby. I couldn't do this again. How the hell could God let this happen to us...AGAIN?*

*We didn't get our miracle. We didn't get our baby. A week later we had a D&C and when I woke up afterwards I was empty. My womb. My heart. I shut down after that. The grief was intense. The pain unimaginable. I was so angry at God. How could He let this happen? If He loved us and was good...WHY DID HE ALLOW BABIES TO DIE AND US TO FEEL THIS PAIN? THIS LOSS.*

*I was consumed by my grief. My anger. I imagine if you could have seen the air around me then it would have been swirling angry reds and black. A storm I held around me like a cloak. I found comfort in the raging of my heart. It was easier to be angry then to deal with the pain in my heart. The loss. It isn't just the loss of that sweet baby you never get to hold. It's more. It's the loss of that first smile. Those first steps. The first "I love you." The first day of school. Riding a bike. Playing sports. Drawing pictures. High School. Prom. College. Falling in love. Weddings. Grandbabies. The loss of a future full of possibilities.*

*It was six months before I spoke to God with anything other than anger. When I finally found the strength to hand over that cloak of red and black and give it to Him. To allow His love and sweet peace to heal me. His Word doesn't promise us that life will be without trials...on the contrary it tells us life with Him will be full of them. It wasn't His plan for us to lose either of those sweet babies. His words says that He "came that they may have and* enjoy life and have it in abundance (to the full, till it overflows.)" John 10:10 AMP

I truly believe it grieved Him as much if not more, since He knew their futures, when they were lost to this world. They will never know the evils of this world. The heartache. The pain. They will only know His glory, His grace, His love and His amazing presence. I WILL get to hold them one day. I WILL get to kiss their faces. I WILL get to learn them. Know them. I find solace in that.

They say that time heals all wounds...I don't really think it's time. It's Him that does the healing. His presence truly is a healing balm. Even though my wounds are healed I'll carry those scars forever. But not as a badge of my pain...but as a reminder of the joy that awaits me when I meet my babies in heaven.

Take heart in Him. I clung to His word, "That I would be a joyful mother of children" (My paraphrase of Psalms 113:9). "That I would not cast my fruit before it's time" (My paraphrase of Malachi 3:11), and that "None of his people would be barren" (My paraphrase of Deuteronomy 7:14). These were my mantras. My prayers. Ella, the fruit of our faith, was born in April 2006, three years after we lost our first baby. He. Is. Faithful.

~ **Katie Keene**, is an Associate Pastor's wife in Lexington, Kentucky and a joyful mother of three children, 10, 7, and 5, and a not so joyful mother of an ornery geriatric black Lab and mostly white Calico cat. Hair. Everywhere.

# Mark's Story

My wife's greatest desire was to be a wife and mother. She'd never had big career aspirations. Her primary aspiration was to be a mother to our children. Her nurturing instinct is tremendous. The fact that we agreed to wait five years after being married before we started trying to have kids was a small miracle. When the time came, we started trying and became pregnant relatively soon.

That first miscarriage was a shock. We cried together. I held my wife. I tried to be sensitive. As I look back on it now, I had very little awareness about what my wife was going through. I was sad, of course. But I didn't feel the loss the same way she did. She had carried that baby, however briefly, and it was already very real to her. She was already sacrificing and nurturing the baby. She was already bonded with the baby. For her, it was just a matter of time until she could express the love she already felt to this precious baby. I, on the other hand, had not felt those same emotions. I think as dad's, our nurturing instinct (which is weaker than our wives to begin with!) doesn't really kick in until we see and hold the baby in our arms.

As I discovered, "miscarriage" was an easier term for me with which I could emotionally cope. It doesn't hurt as much as "we lost our baby" or "the baby died before it could reach full term." Miscarriage sounds much more medical and objective to describe something that occurred. What I learned the hard way with that first miscarriage was that my wife felt every bit the loss as if the child had grown to be an adult. A mother doesn't wait for a baby to be born to love their child. That love starts the moment they know there is a new life growing inside them. Therefore, the grief experienced is just as real and intense when a baby is lost before being born.

I wasn't an insensitive jerk. But I was initially puzzled by the intensity of emotion that my wife felt. I gradually learned to empathize with her more and more. I realized that any attempt to "edit" her feelings to what I felt to be more appropriate levels was misplaced and unreasonable. The less I tried to change her emotional state, and instead to comfort and understand, the more I began to feel what she felt. I shed more tears at that point than I did at the initial loss.

After months of healing, emotionally, physically, and spiritually, we were ready to try again. We were praying together and believing God's promises for Katie to be a "joyful mother." It was still emotional as we felt the lingering doubts and concerns from having a miscarriage.

The second miscarriage was more difficult than the first. Partially because we had prayed and believed and found hope, only to have our hearts broken again. The bigger reason it was more difficult for me as because I understood better the pain it caused my wife. Because I understood her pain more, it was more painful and emotional for me as I supported her and dealt with my own grief.

That's probably the biggest lesson I learned through our loss: the grief was very real. Understanding that helped me to better empathize with Katie. At first, I attempted to deny it for myself and for Katie. It was Katie's honesty in coping with her own grief that enabled me to eventually do the same. I learned that loving my wife, even when we experience a situation very differently, is one of the greatest expressions of my love toward her. That love was expressed by understanding her feelings and her response rather than attempting to change them or dismiss them. It took me longer to recognize this than I'd like to admit.

Perhaps our story can help someone else navigate and heal after the dark days of losing a baby. Wives, you might consider giving your man some grace. Remember, I was not a generally insensitive husband. My wife would say quite the opposite, actually. As a man I sincerely did not understand what my wife was experiencing. In my defense, in some ways I couldn't. We experienced the loss in completely different ways, not just emotionally but biologically. It took time to understand. It took time to see and feel through my wife's perspective. Pray for your husband. Use your words to express yourself to him and help him understand. For many men, understanding their own emotions is difficult. It's another level to empathize with yours. Give him time and help him. If that doesn't work, consider seeking help outside your marriage to help navigate this.

Men: You don't know what you don't know. Please, learn from my mistakes. Don't try to change your wife's emotions or dismiss them because you don't know how to help her. She needs you now more than ever. She doesn't need you to fix her. She just needs you to love her, support her, and faithfully be by her side. Give her time. Don't place unrealistic expectations on her about how long it should take her to heal (emotionally, physically, and spiritually). And don't forget to connect with your own emotions and grief. Find someone safe to whom you can talk. Be honest with yourself. Trust Jesus more than anything, because He's the healer and restorer.

Three years after our first miscarriage, Katie gave birth to our first miracle, Ella. She is now 11, and was followed by two brothers, Jack (8) and Hudson (5). God is good. God is faithful. Never lose heart.

~ **Mark Keene**, Associate Pastor, Bethel Harvest Church, Nicholasville, Kentucky

# Rebecca's Story

I think what Michelle is doing is so important for all women going through such a painful and private time in their life. Dealing with infertility might be the most frustrating and disheartening struggle that a couple will ever have to go through. You are empty, sad, and confused. I was fortunate to have friends and clients who had shared their stories with me before I ever went through my own struggles.

But no matter the stories I heard, it would never happen to us. Until it did. Nothing could prepare me for all of the feelings that would consume me AND my husband. For us it was the infertility that took us down. We did get pregnant at one point, but it resulted in a miscarriage very early on. I was having heavy bleeding and I knew something was wrong. Although I was sad, I was at peace. The hardest part was every month when my cycle would start. Why?! And, would I ever get pregnant?! It caused me to pull away from friends and it certainly wasn't easy on my marriage. This wasn't anything that any woman in my family had dealt with, and that made it even more shameful for me. At least a year after our miscarriage, we finally decided it was time to see a fertility specialist. It was such a relief. To us, this was so foreign and embarrassing. To these doctors, it's their normal. They were able to figure out what was going on, and help us conceive our baby boy. This chapter of sadness was finally over.

To all women struggling, don't be afraid to share your story. It helps to talk, and it allows others to open up to you. You might be surprised to find out how many people have been through the same thing. It's also important to know that everyone handles their pain differently. Some with humor and some with tears, but however you feel is the right way. Have faith. It's not always on our timeframe – in fact, it is way better when you can wait for His *timeframe. And when you finally get your baby, all of the pain and sadness turns to the most incredible love that a person could feel. We now have a handsome boy and a darling girl. I wouldn't trade my pain or my story for anything in the world. These babies were worth the wait.*


~ **Rebecca Blackburn**, *Entrepreneur, Business Owner, Mother of Two, Louisville, Kentucky*

# Jennifer's Story

Ten years ago, when I got pregnant with my first child it was so easy -- too easy. The first month we tried to get pregnant, we did. I told everyone as soon as I found out at three weeks. Why wouldn't I? I breezed through that pregnancy without a care in the world. Nine months later, I gave birth to a big, healthy baby boy.

Two years later, we decided to try again, and I quickly became pregnant. I knew right away -- my body ached in just the right way, and I felt incredibly tired. I told everyone who would listen that we were pregnant again. But then something changed, I didn't feel right. The fatigue went away, and I started to feel like my old self. Within a day or two I began spotting and headed to the emergency room.

I was having a miscarriage, the doctors said. I was surprised on how matter-of-fact they all were about it. It happens all the time, they said. Try again, they said. But all I could think about was what did I do wrong? Did I eat something that harmed the baby? Did I do something that would put it in harm's way? You play those scenarios in your head.

I don't know why there's shame and embarrassment surrounding announcing a miscarriage. I guess it makes folks uncomfortable. Since I announced my pregnancy to the world, I had to announce my miscarriage. People really don't know what to say or do. It's "all for the best" is common, but that doesn't make you feel better. How can this be better than having a baby?

A few months later, we got the courage to try again, and boom - pregnant again. This time, we kept our mouths shut for weeks. Why? What if something happened.? At six weeks I was starting to feel comfortable and began opening up to family and my co-workers about the pregnancy. As our eight-week appointment rolled around, I was excited to hear the baby's heartbeat. But as she moved the wand around my belly in silence I knew something was wrong. No heartbeat.

Medical professionals don't mean to be cold, but they certainly can be. The doctor went into options for "taking care" of the miscarriage almost immediately after telling me there was no heartbeat. I could barely hear her. The best option she said was to let nature take its course.

So, for a few days, there I was, going about my daily routine with the knowledge that my baby was no longer alive inside of me. It's the loneliest feeling in the world. Perhaps because no one can see your pregnancy. The aftermath of letting nature take its course was devastating. I hemorrhaged and had to be rushed to the hospital. It terrified my husband and family.

Physically recovering was pretty fast, but emotionally, I was a wreck. The dreams of a second child began to fade. I told my husband no more, that's it. I can't do this again.

After a few months, I decided one last time. Again, I was pregnant without much effort. That was never my problem -- it was staying pregnant. But this time, I made it all the way.

What miscarriage does is takes the joy out of future pregnancies and replaces it with fear. I was fearful my entire pregnancy. Every time I felt a weird pain, if he moved too much, too little, if I started to feel "not pregnant enough," I freaked out. Every time I went to the restroom, I held my breath, hoping that this time wouldn't be the time the spotting would start. This fear lasted even after I had the baby, it was so deep.

I found that surrounding myself with medical care empathetic to my needs helped tremendously. My new doctor was patient and kind. She went out of her way to ensure I was comforted with *the sound of the baby's heart and ordered multiple ultrasounds throughout my pregnancy to assure me I was producing a healthy baby.*

*During the pregnancy, I tried not to get attached. My husband as well -- we hardly talked about the baby. We didn't want to curse it. In fact, we wouldn't agree on a name until after he was delivered.*

*Now, my little Nicholas, my sunshine, is my gift. And I would never have this wonderful, crazy child if my other pregnancies had been successful. This gives me some peace. But, my mind wanders from time to time and thinks about the other two babies. What would they be like today?*

*~ **Jennifer Plummer**, San Antonio, Texas*

# Krystal's Story

*"For I know the plans I have for you," declares the Lord, "plans to prosper you and not to harm you, plans to give you hope and a future."* Jeremiah 29:11 (NIV)

That cold winter night as I looked up into the rare clear Michigan sky and saw the millions of stars, I screamed and pleaded, "God, you made the Heavens and Earth and all these stars, and yet, you have taken the one thing I've waited for all my life away from me! Why!!? What have I done to deserve such a punishment?" Then I turned and walked into the house where I waited for my husband to come home from work and take me to the hospital for the D&C. A "missed miscarriage" is what they told me earlier that day as I lay anxiously on the table to see and hear for the first time the heartbeat of our first child. I knew something was wrong when I heard the technician sigh an ever so slight sigh. Turning off the ultrasound, she told me the doctor would be in to see me soon. Little did I know that this would be the first of many doctors who would come to me with the crushing words, "I'm sorry, Krystal, but..."

My husband and I started trying to have children one year after we were married. We were in our mid-thirties and knew that it could be more difficult the older we got. So, when I saw the "+ sign" on the test that September 2005, I nearly fell down the steps as I ran to give him the great news. We were very careful not to tell anyone too early, so we waited until Thanksgiving. Two weeks later, I was in the doctor's office having my heart ripped from my chest. But we decided to keep trying. Twenty percent of all women suffer miscarriage, right? Surely next time.

After six months without success, I reached out to the first Fertility Clinic for help. After thirteen IUIs (artificial insemination) without success, we were told the Board of Directors of the clinic had decided we were not viable candidates for IVF and they could no longer help us. I had what they called "unexplained infertility." My husband had been tested with positive results, so the issue was with my reproductive system. Before we left the clinic that day, I told the nurse whose name, ironically, was "Angel" that I would get pregnant again and would reach out to her when I did. It would be a year later when I called Angel to make that appointment. I was pregnant. Soon after my visit, I began spotting. I immediately began praying and crying and yelling and screaming...and bleeding...and bleeding. Even the progesterone could not stop God's plan.

This time I decided to take my anger out on Angelina Jolie! Stupid, right? But it seemed so easy for her and the rest of Hollywood who had all the money in the world to fill their life with the joys of children's laughter that I so desired and deserved. Deserved. Funny word. But that is exactly what I thought. I had suffered enough God. I deserve a child. We deserve to be parents. Deserve...opposite of to serve...I had it all wrong. So, I did what any good Christian would do in my situation. I attended Mass each Sunday, went to confession, took Communion, and bargained with God. "Just give me my heart's desire Lord and I'll do anything!"

About a year later, I learned of an IVF clinic in Ann Arbor, Michigan that a friend of mine had great success with after unexplained infertility. The doctor said he would take us on as clients!! I was so thrilled. My husband, the rational one (thank goodness), was more cautious than me, but throughout this tiresome journey he was always very supportive. So, I started down the long process of fertility drugs, daily injections administered by my husband, and the retrieval and transfer process that comes with IVF. I was hopeful and knew this was God's plan! He just needed to show me the right open door that would surely allow us to enter into the magical world of parenthood! My first two cycles resulted in pregnancy followed quickly by two subsequent miscarriages. We had used all of our embryos. So, after much deliberation we started the process again. By the time the fourth transfer took place (the third did not take), I knew immediately if it was going to be a viable pregnancy. Human chorionic gonadotropin (hCG) levels above 100 one-week post transfer equals success. Anything less than 100 would mean a miscarriage. My hCG level was 129!!! In April 2010 our beautiful daughter was born! God is good ALL the time!

Knowing that we had more embryos, I began the IVF process again in late 2010. In 2011 I became pregnant again. This time the hCG level was below 100, but I was "cautiously optimistic". When I heard the heartbeat at eight weeks, I told God, "I'm satisfied Lord, I'm giving this baby to you." Two weeks later, God once again took my child to be with the others. We would try again with the last of the embryos in December 2011 without success.

Through the ups and downs I knew one thing was for sure. For a brief moment in time, I carried our children. I know life begins at conception, so I chose to honor our children and celebrate their lives no matter how brief. Each child has a name: Gabriel, Alex, Bailey, Maria, and Regan. We tried to stay with gender neutral names with the exception of Maria. We knew she was a girl through genetic testing. I have a figurine for each with their name and date I miscarried them written on the bottom. I keep these in my bedroom as a private memorial.

We also have a Christmas ornament for each child, and as we hang them on the tree each year, we say a prayer. We talk openly with our daughter about her brothers and sisters in Heaven, and she knows they are real. She even shared with her Kindergarten class about how she will "see her brothers and sisters one day in Heaven. They died when they were babies." I want her to know she is not alone. She may be an only child on Earth, but she has five siblings waiting to meet, hug and love her for eternity.

One thing I want to share, even though I know it is rarely talked about openly, is the suffering of husbands. The pain of miscarriage is very real for them, too. My husband is a very private person and prides himself on being the strong arm on which I rely. But I will tell you his tears fell right along with mine and his heart broke with each passing. Many nights he just held me as we sat on our steps as I questioned why. Never once did he offer an explanation. He just held me and told me things would be okay. Of course, he was right. One day we will walk arm in arm as we watch our angels dance in Heaven with our daughter.

I often get questioned as to how I dealt with the losses over the years. My answer has always been that God is good ALL the time. My whole life has been one in which I had to rely on the shelter of His arms. I have no choice. I am His and He is mine. God bless.

~ **Krystal Strasser**, Northville, Michigan

## Jordan's Story

Ever since I was a little girl, I dreamed of being a mommy. I remember being on vacation in high school with my family. I remember not having the best time, because all my friends were chasing boys around. I remember my mom talking to my dad about me. She said, "Jordan will be at her happiest when she can bring her own family and kids on vacation." Which was so true. I was not made for high school, I was not made for college, I was made for becoming a wife and a mom.

I met my husband when I was twenty, he was just eighteen. We got married two years after that, with some disapproval from some because we were young. I knew I wanted to start a family as soon as we could. So, we began trying. We tried for about a year and nothing was happening. I knew something was wrong, after all it shouldn't take this long. We went to the doctor and had some tests ran and were told that we would never be able to make a baby without medical help and even then, it may not happen.

We swallowed that hard pill and decided to continue on with the life we had for a while without diving into fertility help just yet. Then the following summer, we attempted three IUI's. In the world of all things fertility, this is a low level medical intervention, but has a decent success rate depending on your fertility issues. All three failed. We were back at square one. We decided to take a year off because financially we couldn't even attempt the next step.

The following summer we started IVF. We did our first procedure in September. Five days following the procedure, I got a faint positive pregnancy test. Ten days later blood work confirmed that I was in fact pregnant. We were over the moon. We had never, in our three years of trying, seen those glorious two pink lines. Eight days after my blood work, I started bleeding in the middle of the night. I knew right away we were losing the baby. I did not need a doctor to confirm this to me, I felt it. We were in limbo for a week after that, because my body was trying to miscarry the baby but was in no hurry to do so.

Angry is the only word that comes to mind when I think of our miscarriage. I kept questioning God. Why would He even allow me to become pregnant if He was just going to take the baby away? Why allow me to feel that excitement, only to strip it from my womb? I was mad at God and I was mad at my body.

After miscarrying, my desire to be a mom only intensified. I did not give myself time to absorb my feelings, nor did I give my husband that time. I knew I wanted to be a mom, and I wanted to as soon as possible. So as soon as my doctor cleared me for another procedure, I knew we were doing it.

December 10th, 2015, I had that next procedure. I got pregnant again. But this time I wouldn't allow myself to get excited for a long time. "TWINS!", is what they told us at my eight-week appointment. We were so excited, but secretly I was even more scared. Twins puts more stress on your body, and I did not want to lose either of them.

Elijah and Amiah were growing on track and were healthy babies. My pregnancy was blissful, joy-filled, and easy. Until June 12th. I was twenty-nine weeks pregnant when I thought my water had broken. I called my husband and said I was going to labor and delivery because I thought my water had broken but did not worry him because I also said maybe I just peed myself. (Because that happens when you have two babies sitting on your bladder.) ☺ I get to the hospital and they confirm that yes, my water had broken. But I was not worried because often women pregnant with twins go into pre-term labor and they can try and hold it off for a bit. I also was five weeks past viability, so I knew if they were born they had a pretty good chance still.

They immediately hooked me up to monitors to monitor Elijah and Amiah's hearts. They found each heartbeat, or so we thought. About three hours later, I had to use the restroom, so they had to take the monitors off. Once they went to put them back on, they could not find one of the twins' heartbeat. The doctor brought in the ultrasound machine. He found Elijah's heartbeat right away, we saw it. He put the wand over Amiah, and I knew. After twenty-plus ultrasounds during my pregnancy, I knew what a beating heart looked like. I knew right away hers was not beating. He said he was going to get the better ultrasound machine that had better image quality. So, repeat again. Nothing. He looked up at me and my husband, and then he looked over at our parents (who had come up to the hospital following the news that I would be stuck in the hospital) and asked them to leave the room.

He confirmed what I already knew. Amiah's heart had stopped beating. She was gone. That was the worst moment of my life. I didn't sleep that night. I just stared at the wall. I had such a range of emotions. I was in shock. I didn't understand. I wanted them to take Elijah out, because apparently my body was not the safest place for my babies. My body didn't fight for Amiah, my body let her go.

I stayed pregnant for four more weeks. I was induced at 34 weeks and delivered both of my babies. One came out screaming, and the other came out lifeless. That was the most conflicting day of emotions I have ever had. I was so beyond filled with joy over my son. But I was so sorrow filled and hopeless over my stillborn daughter.

We spent time with Amiah before they took her away. I admired her little toes and wondered of all the places those feet would have taken her. I gazed into her sweet face, picturing what her smile would have looked like. I held her tiny hands and thought of all the lives she would have touched with her own. I selfishly told God that she would have been safer with me than with Him, which I know isn't true. I was envious of God, and all the time He was going to get with my Amiah before I did.

So here I am, six months after hearing Amiah's heart stopped beating and five months after my twins were born. I am still learning to deal with the loss of my daughter. I still teeter between living life and mourning her death. I take comfort in knowing she is with Jesus. I truly do not know how people make it through deaths of children without knowing our Savior.

Often, I found myself shutting out the emotions my soul needed to feel amidst the death of my daughter. I kept choosing to stay busy with her brother, or my husband or work. But I knew I needed to fully grieve her. She deserves that. She deserves every part of my heart, even the sorrow filled pieces. So, I take it day by day, I allow myself to feel what I need to. Even if that means breaking down over something small. I am allowed to feel this way.

Acknowledging Amiah helps me so much. I say her name often. I love when others want to talk about Amiah with me. She was here, and she left a very large and real footprint on so many. It would not be fair to only talk about Elijah. She is just as much my child as Elijah is.

Amiah will always be my first daughter, even if we go on to have more children. I will always remember her. Some days are better than others. I trust that Jesus is in Heaven telling Amiah all about her family. How we love her so well, how her Daddy is such a goofball, how her Mommy would do anything to snuggle her just one more time, and how her brother wishes his sister was *here. Even though Amiah was taken from me, I do not ever regret that she was made. I am grateful for every moment I had with*

*her, even though it was far too short of a time. We will see you again, my sweet, sweet angel.*

- **Jordan Sanders**, *Teacher and Founder of the Amiah Mae Foundation, Lexington, Kentucky*

# *Kevin's Story*

My Perspective on a Journey through a Difficult Emotional and Physical Period for Brenda...

*God placed Brenda in my life and we were married for over twenty-six years. Before we were married, Brenda shared her painful memories of the most traumatic experience of her short life. As a nineteen-year-old young woman, she made a decision to abort a child due to fear of dissatisfaction from her parents, a potential inability to finish college, and the difficulties of raising a child as a single parent. There were significant consequences to that decision that would impact Brenda's life forever.*

*As Brenda's relationship with Jesus Christ deepened, she felt immense remorse over the abortion decision. The feeling was so overwhelming and powerful, she made a strong commitment to use whatever time on earth she had remaining to help other women make a different choice...a choice for life. I watched her intensity level rise each day driven by a desire to "make up" for what she called her biggest mistake. She joined an organization called Operation Rescue, a pro-life group that would hand out literature in front of abortion clinics, pray for the women in a crisis pregnancy, and, at times, physically block entrances to the clinics. In fact, one-year Brenda and other members of Operation Rescue were arrested for the latter activity.*

*Throughout this time, Brenda would often cry about the past and other women who made the choice to abort their child. It was difficult to console Brenda and even fully understand Brenda's emotions, but I would try to encourage her to follow her passion to help others without forgetting that God has forgiven her just* as He forgives each of us for every sin. However, Brenda was not free from the guilt of the abortion until her final year on earth.

To reinforce the guilt, five years into our marriage Brenda was unable to conceive, and after a series of infertility tests, it was determined that there was a slight possibility of a successful pregnancy if the "in vitro" fertilization method was used. The thought of potentially having a "frozen" embryo was almost as terrifying emotionally as the abortion, given the fetus would be in a suspended state and life halted, waiting until maybe someday the life would be resumed. So, the decision was made to abandon pursuit of a biological child and pursue adoption instead.

The adoption process was filled with many emotional ups and downs. The emotional volatility was almost unbearable to Brenda given her innate desire to become a mother combined with the guilt of the past. She made a plea to God that she would be relentless in her role as mother if He blessed her with a child. I have no doubt God intervened in our lives as He opened the doors to four adoptions.

Brenda wanted to please God and show Him that she was infinitely thankful, so the rest of her life on earth was dedicated to the children. We homeschooled them, and Brenda had a very intense focus on them twenty-four seven. This was not a bad thing, but it was obvious that she was driven by the desire to "make up" for the past. In fact, her enormous drive sometimes overtook her ability to love and enjoy the blessings of the children God provided. For example, she knew putting God's Word in our children's heart would impact their life and eternity. Bible memorization was a must and was not only encouraged but required. This is not a bad thing, but often the message was delivered in a militaristic manner rather than with love. So, my role was to inject some balance which was sometimes perceived as counterproductive given what was defined as the goal and the *thought that nothing should come close to knocking us off the course toward achieving the goal.*

*The final chapter of Brenda's life on earth began with the words she received from her doctor that she had an aggressive form of breast cancer, that it had metastasized to various places in her body, and likely had six months or so of life left, even if treated with aggressive measures. Brenda passed away two-and-a-half years after first hearing of the disease in her body after a valiant, courageous, and determined effort to fight.*

*I know the strength she demonstrated came from two sources. The first was realizing that God could heal her. The second was motivation to continue to carry out her dedication to raising the children she was blessed with, which was her commitment to God. As her husband, I often wondered what I could do to help. Men typically like to fix things and I began to realize that it is impossible for me to "fix" the problem other than to take Brenda to many doctors, read up on the subject to gain a better understanding of what could be done to extend her life, assist her in making a multitude of medical procedure decisions, and be the emotional support for Brenda and our children during this extremely difficult time.*

*A popular line of thinking is that men generally have less emotional swings and that emotional stability is what makes men a helpmate to a woman. However, emotional distress from extreme circumstances will affect all human beings. I was not immune to this. The stress that resulted from the emotional distress affected Brenda in a way that her burden was never light. This would often force me to try to understand exactly what she was feeling so that I could find the key to unlocking her emotional bondage so that she could enjoy life, regardless of how long she would have remaining on earth. This was a daily task. My battle was to remain focused on Brenda and not my own thoughts, feelings, and emotional pain. To help Brenda and the children* through this time, I would not reveal my stress or feelings of sadness, anxiety, or even at times, uncertainty about how long Brenda would be on earth.

After Brenda died, I settled into one of the darkest periods of my life. The children were my top priority, and I was focused on leading them where they should go but overlooked their emotions. A couple of years later, God provided another companion for life. He restored my joy, He blessed me with more children, and He began to untangle the knotted emotions that I had, and my older children experienced. That work is not finished, but God has provided much wisdom. The lessons learned are invaluable, which is always the case when your teacher is the Maker of the Universe.

*~ Kevin Sheehan, Versailles, KY*

## Hope's Story

I'm sure there are millions of women out there that have experienced a forced miscarriage, and the pain and trauma that are experienced. Unfortunately, we have silenced these lonely victims of miscarriage, because it's too difficult to talk about. So, when you add to it, the fact that my babies were forcibly miscarried during sex trafficking, it's drowned out completely. The pain is being muffled like my mouth, as I was being raped repeatedly. Since I was born into sex slavery, I was a commodity. When I got pregnant it was an unwanted pregnancy to my traffickers.

I had never bonded with any human, because there wasn't anyone safe enough to bond to. So, I didn't know how to bond to the baby growing in my belly. Still today, it's difficult to say, "my baby", because the loss of a child is unbearable. In order to cope, I saw them as "a baby" not "my baby". As your child grows in your belly you can't help but attach, the Holy Spirit flows freely between the baby and their mother and causes an unbreakable bond. There is genuine love, acceptance, a small tiny being relying on you for survival. I couldn't stop feeling hope as I carried the children that would shortly be taken from me. Life brings confident expectation of good, and in the hell of what I was experiencing a glimmer of love was in my belly. I still haven't grieved fully, to be honest, I have grieved countless things over the thirteen years of my healing journey. But the loss of a child is deep, it's gut wrenching.

There was intense guilt that went along with the miscarriages. It was because they told me I was so evil the babies couldn't live in my body. I rejected myself, and my body because I thought it was my fault they died. Satan used lie after lie to get me to hate myself deeper. Satan steals, kills, and destroys, he is *the father of lies. No matter what form the lie is presented in, it is incapacitating.*

*As I was healing, the Lord brought truth to the lies, including the lie that it was my fault. Papa God showed me a vision of my children in heaven waiting for me. They are so happy, they are so peaceful! Papa God showed me how they just want me to live fully, and to not be in pain. Since that is their heart desire I make a choice each day that I will live fully. I make a choice each day for my babies and myself, that I will live a life of joy and expectation for the day I will finally see them face to face!*

~ ***Hope Beryl-Green***

MICHELLE RENÉE CHUDY

# Your Story

## Time to Heal

*There is a time for everything, and a season for every activity under heaven: a time to be born and a time to die, a time to plant and a time to uproot, a time to kill and a time to heal, a time to tear down and a time to build, a time to weep and a time to laugh, a time to mourn and a time to dance, a time to scatter stones and a time to gather them, a time to embrace and a time to refrain, a time to search and a time to give up, a time to keep and a time to throw away, a time to tear and a time to mend, a time to be silent and a time to speak, a time to love and a time to hate, a time for war and a time for peace. What does the worker gain from his toil? I have seen the burden God has laid on men. He has made everything beautiful in its time. He has also set eternity in the hearts of men; yet they cannot fathom what God has done from beginning to end.*
*Ecclesiastes 3:1-11 (NIV)*

There really is a season for everything, good and bad. What you are going through is important. And you have to go *through*...because what's important is on the other side. Don't get stuck in the valley!

There comes an appointed time when the season is over, and you must move on. That includes grieving; however, how you move is up to you. Emotional and mental healing is optional. You must choose to pursue healing and receive it. Rest assured that healing is not forgetting. It doesn't erase your memories, healing makes them bearable and qualifies you to help others who are suffering from the same.

Psalm 147:3 says, He heals the brokenhearted and binds up their wounds. Jesus wants you healed even from the deepest wound of losing your child. Grief and sorrow are not meant to be carried past their season. The end must be declared before the new can begin. And from that new place of healing you can provide comfort to others with the same comfort He has given you (2 Corinthians 1: 3-4).

The following exercises are tools designed to help you work through the visible and hidden effects of miscarriage. It's a process used in life coaching to deal with the source of pain. The benefits come when you honestly invest yourself in the process. As you complete them, be real, be transparent and hold nothing back.

The exercises must be done in the order listed. ***To receive the full benefit, do not skip any of the steps and be as detailed as possible.*** Remember it is a process, and you are working through levels of pain and grief. The harder it is to do, the more you need to do it. Your healing begins with your first step toward the Healer. And each step you take, brings you closer to comfort and the restoration of joy.

**Please note these exercises are not a substitute for professional counseling.** If you are dealing with the heaviness of depression, uncontrolled emotions or thoughts, or if you just need to talk, please reach out for professional help. Counseling is a wonderful resource. A godly counselor can help you navigate the way to healing and restored emotional health. My seasons in counseling were the best gift God ever gave me. So, in honor of your heaven born child or children, let's begin your journey of healing...turn the page and take your first step.

---

*"When life feels dreadfully dark and you can't see a single fleck of light, maybe it's not too far a reach to think perhaps God could have you in a crevice covered with His hand. He will be good to you, but it is possible to be blind to His goodness until the blackness has ended. In the wording of Exodus 33:23, sometimes you may only see His back."[5]*
*Beth Moore*

---

## Grief Healing Exercises

*Resources Needed:*

- *Notebook or Journal*
- *Pen*
- *Bible*
- *Tissues*
- *Private Quiet Location*
- *Approximately 2-3 Hours*

Before you begin, I need to ask...*do you struggle hearing the voice of God?* Better yet, *do you hear His voice at all?* I know this is often a source of angst especially when you are desperate for an answer or a touch from Him. I'd like to bless you with the gift of hearing Him. The following steps have helped me discern God's voice. If you are in a place where you can't hear Him or not sure if He is speaking to you, the following are *Four Keys to Hearing God's Voice.* [6,7]

- **Be Still.** *Quiet yourself down and minimize distractions. His voice is like the sound of many waters, but He speaks to us in a still quiet voice. A busy noisy life can drown out His sweet words, if we're not careful.*

- **Vision.** *Keep your eyes on Jesus. Picture Him in your mind and focus on Jesus.*

- **Spontaneity.** *Be attentive to spontaneous thoughts or thoughts that are outside of what you are thinking. The* *best example is you are thinking one line of thought, and a thought intersects yours. That is His voice! Note that His voice always aligns with the Bible. He will never go against His Word.*

- ***Journal.*** *Record what He is saying and your thoughts, as well. He wants a two-way dialogue. What you are writing is your conversation with God.*

Now grab a notebook and pen, find a quiet place, and give yourself approximately three hours of uninterrupted time. Be sure to turn off your mobile devices or anything that distracts you. It is ideal for you to complete all the steps in the same sitting. **Complete the writing assignments by hand and not computer.** This is a must! A computer or device allows you to detach from your emotions as you compose on screen.

Follow the instructions of each step, and address the specific items listed. Include details and stay within the noted boundaries for each assignment. Each step is an instrument of healing geared to reveal what is hidden and wants to hold you in your grief. *Please note it is not necessary to share the letters with the people addressed for you to receive the benefit from writing them.* They are meant for your healing, and the exercises are between you and God.

So, let the healing begin…

## The Healing Journey

### Step 1 ~ **Prayer & Declaration**

Start with prayer. Specifically ask the Holy Spirit to help you and to bring to your mind all that needs to be addressed. Tell Jesus that you are ready to be healed and thank Him now for healing you.

*Declare: It's time for me to heal.*

### Step 2 ~ **Miscarriage Autobiography**

Write a letter about your personal miscarriage experience and ***every painful event*** associated with it. If it hurt you physically, mentally or emotionally, write about it. If you've had more than one miscarriage, please treat each loss as unique and discuss each one. Write down any memory that the Holy Spirit reveals even if it's silly or doesn't make sense. If it comes to you, don't discount it, write it down. Let your writing flow in the order it's given. Don't try to control or be concerned about how it reads or appears. This is between you and God. Please sign and date your letter.

## *Step 3* ~ **Identify Offenders**

Review your autobiography and identify all the sources of your pain (offenders). Possible offenders could be people or an organization (hospital, workplace, or church). Again, try to identify the actual source. Make a list starting with the worst offender (primary offender) and work down to the least. Remember pain can result by commission or omission. If their actions or words (or lack thereof) hurt you, the source of the pain is considered an offender. It is imperative that you validate your pain. Remember this is a healing exercise and your pain must be acknowledged.

## *Step 4* ~ **Offender Letters**

Write a letter to each offender starting with the primary offender. Include the ***specific pain or hurt*** they caused ***you*** and ***express how it made you feel***. Do not make excuses on their behalf or deny the pain. If it hurt you, write it down. Don't be surprised or afraid if God ends up on your list. He did on mine. He already knows how we feel, so it isn't a surprise to Him. Follow this pattern in your letter:

(OFFENDER'S NAME) DID/SAID (OFFENSE), AND IT MADE ME FEEL (EMOTION)

(OFFENDER'S NAME) DIDN'T DO/SAY (OFFENSE), AND IT MADE ME FEEL (EMOTION)

If God is one of your offenders, please pray before writing Him and ask Him to speak while you write. Be brutally honest in your letter to Him. Listen for His voice as you write and record His response. Sign and date your letter. *Again, these letters are only for personal healing use and not intended for confrontation.*

## Step 5 ~ **Accountability Letter**

Take a moment to pray and reflect over the offender letters. Ask the Lord to show you the truth. Consider if your *response* to the pain they caused you was considered sin in God's eyes. Make a list of those sins to include unforgiveness. God considers it a sin when we don't forgive others and it must be confessed. Bitterness is also a common response to offense and is also considered a sin. Ask the Lord to reveal any root of bitterness. Now write a letter to each offender taking responsibility for your reaction to their offense that *wasn't godly*. Sign and date your letter.

## Step 6 ~ **God Letter**

Write a letter to God and thank Him for healing your wounds. Confess to Him any hurt or hopelessness you've held against Him, and the sins revealed in the accountability letter. Ask Him to specifically forgive you of bitterness and unforgiveness toward Him or any person you wrote an accountability letter. Acknowledge His ways are higher, and you will no longer try to understand and will rest in His sovereign will. Entrust your child to Him and thank Him for caring for your baby for the rest of eternity. Sign and date your letter.

## Step 7 ~ **Baby Letter**

Write a letter to your baby expressing your love. Tell them how much you miss them and everything that you long to say. Let them know that you're okay with Father God caring for them until you enter heaven and are reunited. Ensure your baby that you will be with them again one day. If you haven't yet given your baby a name, I'd encourage you to do so. If you're not sure of the gender, pray and ask the Lord to let you know. Trust that He will not lead you astray. Name your sweet baby and sign and date your letter.

## Step 8 ~ **Your Love Letter**

Refer to Step 4 and note the Scripture or words God spoke to you while writing His offender letter. Write a letter **addressed to yourself,** but note it is written by God to you. If He gave you Scripture in Step 4, wrap a sentence around the Scripture. Sign the letter "Love Abba" and date it. Now read the letter out loud to yourself by starting with "Dear Beloved (Insert Your Name).

## *Step 9* ~ **Validation of Life**

Part of the misery of miscarriage is lack of closure. Most of us didn't have the opportunity to lay our child to rest or validate their life through a wake or funeral. From the day your baby was conceived, he or she lived. Their life matters and is worthy of celebration and remembrance.

A special place has been prepared for you to honor and commemorate your baby. Visit **Heaven Born Babes** Facebook page at **fb.me/HeavenBabes**, and post a message about your baby or to your baby. If you have an ultrasound or photo, share that, too. **Heaven Born Babes** is a healing wall and living testament of our babies who left us with aching hearts, empty arms, and a forever love that binds us into eternity. It's a place to publicly validate their life and our love. The wall is a memorial dedicated to our heavenly babes.

## You're Invited

There are many blessings I pray you received through **Song of the Barren**...comfort, validation, laughter, healing, hope, and community, just to name a few. But I want to make sure you receive the greatest gift of all, and that is a relationship with Jesus as your Lord and Savior. It is a relationship with Him alone that opens the door to heaven and everlasting life. Without Him we are all bound for hell. It's His desire that none perish, and just one sin separates us from God unless Jesus steps into our life and redeems it.

You can guarantee that you will see your heaven born babe and live in heaven eternally by calling on Jesus as LORD and repenting of sin. Salvation is a free gift to all who believe, and it only requires childlike faith to receive. If you have never accepted Christ as your personal Lord and Savior, it is as simple as **ABC**.

**A**dmit that Jesus Christ is God's only Son and your sin separates you from God. **B**elieve that Jesus died for your sins, rose again, and is now seated at God the Father's right hand. **C**onfess that Jesus is your Savior, invite Him to be LORD of your life and turn from your sin. It's through relationship with Jesus alone that is the door to God the Father and heaven. If you would like to ask Jesus to be your Savior, please pray the following prayer:

*Dear Jesus, You are the Christ! I confess that I'm a sinner and choose to turn from my sin through repentance. I believe You are the only one who can save me and give me eternal life. I believe You are God's only Son who died for my sins in my place, rose from the grave and now sit in heaven at God's right hand. I want a relationship with you and ask you to be LORD of my life. I surrender all of my life to You. Please fill me with Your Holy Spirit, so I can live for You. Amen.*

If you just prayed the prayer above, congratulations and welcome to God's family! Your name is now written in the Lamb's Book of Life and you are in a salvation covenant with Jesus. I'd love to know about your decision so please drop me a note at saved@michellechudy.com. I also encourage you to check out https://michellechudy.com/about/knowhim/ for more information on how to grow in your relationship with Him.

To help you on your journey with Jesus and to get you growing in your life's purpose, I'd like to bless you with my three-category #1 bestselling book **The House of You: Built for a Purpose. Structured for His Plan.** Please go to this link to get your free eBook: http://bit.ly/SongHouseofYou

Blessings,

## Your Notes

## Resources

Whether you've suffered through miscarriage or support someone who has, though not an exhaustive list, the following resources are available to help facilitate healing. If overwhelmed by your loss, please note that professional counseling and/or Grief Share Ministries are fabulous resources to help you navigate the grief.

- Educational Postcards
    - http://www.throughtheheart.org/educational-postcards/
- Comfort Kits
    - http://www.throughtheheart.org/about/
- The Compassionate Friends
    - https://www.compassionatefriends.org/
- Discussion Forums
    - http://throughtheheart1.proboards.com/
- Facebook Communities
    - https://www.facebook.com/HeavenBabes/
    - https://www.facebook.com/miscarriagemiracles/
- Grief Counselor or Therapist
- Grief Share Classes
- Healing Through Art
    - http://www.throughtheheart.org/healing-through-art/
- **Heaven Born Babes – Healing Wall**
    - https://www.facebook.com/HeavenBabes/

- Men's Resources:
    - https://grievingdads.com/blog/
    - http://www.pregnancybirthbaby.org.au/fathers-and-miscarriage
    - http://raisingchildren.net.au/articles/miscarriage_dads.html
    - https://www.tommys.org/our-organisation/about-us/charity-news/dads-feel-heartbreak-miscarriage-too
- National Suicide Prevention Lifeline 1.800.273.8255
- Pastoral Counseling
- Photography
    - https://www.nowilaymedowntosleep.org/
- Pregnancy Loss Support & Education
    - *Through the Heart:* http://www.throughtheheart.org
    - *Faces of Loss, Faces of Hope:* http://facesofloss.com/
    - *Share Pregnancy & Infant Loss Support:* http://nationalshare.org/
- Your Physician
- Workplace Wellness Programs

## Afterword

In the United States, one in four women experience miscarriage in their life. That is two thousand women per day, 700,000 per year – one-fourth of all females in this country – who lose a baby to pregnancy/infant loss.[8]

In the United States a miscarriage is usually defined as loss of a baby before the twentieth week of pregnancy, and a stillbirth is loss of a baby after twenty weeks of pregnancy.[9]

Unfortunately, between ten and twenty-five percent of known pregnancies end in miscarriage, and eighty percent happen in the first trimester.[10]

Stillbirth effects about one percent of all pregnancies, and each year about 24,000 babies are stillborn in the United States.[11]

Sadly, most survivors don't disclose their loss mostly because society hasn't given permission. It's an uncomfortable topic. They reenter every-day-life without pause to mourn or admittance of loss, and weep in silence for years. Silence masks the well of devastation and hopelessness. The emotional, psychological and physical impacts are often dealt with in isolation. Miscarriage survival is a difficult conversation to have, but a necessary one for those coping with the grief. To provide necessary support and resources to those in need there must be education, awareness, but mostly acknowledgement of the depth of grief.

So, how do you help? What can be done to facilitate the healing process? **Break the silence.** Whether as a friend, family member, workplace environment or church organization, you can be an agent of healing by offering a safe place to grieve. An attempt to understand can validate the need of support and start the recovery journey. For a church, workplace or organization, consider offering pregnancy loss outreach, support services or ministries. Include miscarriage and stillbirth specialized curriculum in existing grief recovery programs, offer a current list of recommended counselors and reading materials.

When establishing a miscarriage outreach ministry or support services, consider the following list. It is not inclusive, but it's a starting point. The best way to develop or grow your program, is to get direct feedback from miscarriage survivors. Ask both the mother, father, and siblings what they needed or would have appreciated during their time of grief:

- *Baby Item Returns and/or Storage*
- *Baby Keepsake*
- *Condolence Cards/Letters*
- *Educational & Encouragement Materials*
- *Family Meal Service*
- *Grief Counselors*
- *Grief Journals*
- *House Cleaning*
- *Memorial Service*

- *Mentor/Accountability Partner*
- *Naming Ceremony*
- *Ongoing Prayer Chain*
- *Online Forums*
- *Sibling Care*
- *Support Groups*

## Song of the Barren

## Author's Note

Thank you for reading *Song of the Barren: Miscarriages to Miracles*.

I pray you found not only comfort, but hope. Your thoughts matter to me and your book review is greatly appreciated!

Please take a moment to leave a review on Amazon, my store at www.michellechudy.com and applicable sites. Stop by **@miscarriagemiracles** on Facebook and "*like*" and "*share*" the ***Song of the Barren*** page. Spread the word on Twitter, Instagram, and Pinterest, too. Help me sow seeds of awareness of miscarriage loss, and bring healing and hope to those who mourn.

God Bless,

Michelle Chudy is a #1 Bestselling Author, International Business Trainer, and Certified Business and Life Coach. She helps Christian professionals define their niche, sharpen their brand, and identify market opportunities so they can breakthrough market barriers!

To learn more about Michelle and her writings visit her site www.michellechudy.com, and follow her on Facebook, Instagram and Twitter. To purchase her bestselling book **The House of You** in print, buy it now at http://amzn.to/2m4JakB. You can also buy her autobiography of **The Battle of Surrender: One Woman's Journey to Sacrifice** in audible format on Amazon.com http://amzn.to/2Ejfms6, or get it in ebook or a signed print copy at https://michellechudy.com/store/.

FIGURE 34: MY HEART - MY WORLD
AUTHOR MICHELLE CHUDY, HUSBAND MARK CHUDY, DAUGHTERS
HAIDYN & CARIS CHUDY, & FUR BABIES ZACH & ZOEY

## Notes to Text

[1] Beth Moore, *Perfect Timing, Jesus 90 Days with the One and Only,* (Nashville: B&H Publishing Group, 2007), 29.

[2] Derek Prince, *Found on the Rock-Part 2,* Derek Prince Ministries, television broadcast, God TV, 3 September 2009.

[3] Dr. Seuss, *Oh, the Places You'll Go,* (New York: Random House, 1990).

[4] Todd Burpo with Lynn Vincent, *Heaven is For Real,* (Nashville: Thomas Nelson, 2010).

[5] Beth Moore, *The Quest, An Excursion Toward Intimacy With God,* (Nashville: LifeWay® Press, 2017), 80.

[6] Mark Virkler, *4 Keys to Hearing God's Voice" Mark Virkler Pt.1,* Communion with God Ministries, YouTube https://youtu.be/oqvi8-86Rak, 18 July 2012.

[7] Mark Virkler, *4 Keys to Hearing God's Voice" Mark Virkler Pt.2,* Communion with God Ministries, YouTube https://youtu.be/SwkSHuuig3k, 18 July 2012.

[8] Wired, *National Pregnancy and Infant Loss Awareness Day: I am 1 in 4,* https://www.wired.com/2011/10/national-pregnancy-and-infant-loss-awareness-day-i-am-1-in-4/, 15 October 2011.

[9] Centers for Disease Control and Prevention, *Facts about Stillbirth,* https://www.cdc.gov/ncbddd/stillbirth/facts.html, 2 October 2017.

[10] Healthline, *A Breakdown of Miscarriage by Week,* https://www.healthline.com/health/pregnancy/miscarriage-rates-by-week#3, 20 January 2016.

[11] Macdorman MF, Gregory ECW. Fetal and perinatal mortality, United States, 2013. National vital statistics reports; vol 64 no 8. Hyattsville, MD: National Center for Health Statistics. 2015.

www.ingramcontent.com/pod-product-compliance
Lightning Source LLC
LaVergne TN
LVHW051555070426
835507LV00021B/2595